GOOD SPORTS
JOKE BOOK

Compiled by
Paul M. Miller

BARBOUR
PUBLISHING

THE GOOD SPORTS
JOKE BOOK

Cover illustration by Dave Garbot.

Published by Barbour Publishing, Inc., P.O. Box 719, Uhrichsville, Ohio 44683, www.barbourbooks.com

Our mission is to publish and distribute inspirational products offering exceptional value and biblical encouragement to the masses.

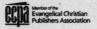 Member of the
Evangelical Christian
Publishers Association

Printed in the United States of America.
5 4 3 2 1

CONTENTS

INTRODUCTION:
RUNS, HITS, AND
(NOT MANY) ERRORS

All good sports know, as Proverbs 17:22 says, "A cheerful heart [and a well-thrown fastball] is good medicine."

Of all the clichés and homilies found in the lexicon of sport, none is quoted more often than "It isn't whether you win or lose, it's how you play the game that counts." You tell that to an eager rookie or a been-around-the-bases-a few-thousand-times pro, and they'll both laugh and say something like, "Yeah, you tell that joke to our boss upstairs."

Sports stories have also been ammunition for those who speak for The Man Upstairs. They know that the common playing field of good sportsmanship applies to this season and all the seasons of eternity. Sometimes a good laugh is the best way to get the point across.

Remember this knee-slapper? Q: Who was the first athlete mentioned in the Bible? A: Joseph; he served in Pharaoh's court. That little number used to bring down the house in places of worship and Sunday school classes. But there's no doubt that that whizbanger has been shelved, right alongside the road-crossing chicken and the fireman's red suspenders.

What this collection of sports humor for every season has going for it is the scope of its contents. While you may not find your favorite lacrosse joke here, you'll certainly find a plethora of jock humor that'll give you a good-sport edge in the locker room as well as in your Sunday school class.

BASEBALL

Wasn't it Yogi Berra who said, "You can observe a lot by just watching"? Maybe that's why baseball is called the great American pastime. There are so many people observing. And what do they probably see? The weirdness of a multi-million-dollar pitcher who needs relief. Figure that one out, Yogi.

BASEBALL IN HEAVEN

For their entire lives, Phil and Tony lived baseball. They went to more than sixty games a year. They even agreed that whoever died first would come back and tell the other if there was a ball diamond in heaven.

One night in the middle of a Yankees game, Phil passed on happy. A few nights later, Tony awoke to Phil's voice coming from the beyond. "Phil, is that you?"

"Of course it's me."

"Quick, tell me," Tony excitedly asked, "is there baseball in heaven?"

"First the good news. Yes, Tony, there

is baseball in heaven."

"And the bad news?"

"You're pitching tomorrow night."

CHEW ON THIS

Jake: Our town's baseball league is the worst!

Jock: How bad is it?

Jake: It's so bad the kids throw away the baseball cards and collect the bubble gum.

BASEBALL ONE-LINERS

I was watching a baseball game on television when my wife said, "Speaking of high and outside, the grass needs mowing."

The only problem he has in the outfield is with fly balls.

That free agent doesn't steal bases, he buys them.

He's such a tough hitter he even gets walks at batting practice.

I like the good old days when umpires called strikes and the player's union didn't.

Our team was so bad that when they played the National Anthem, the flag was at half-staff.

The only thing that stays in the cellar longer than those losers is a furnace.

Baseball will outlast all other sports because a diamond is forever.

Old ball players never die; they're just debased.

LITTLE LEAGUE

No wonder kids are so confused these days. I saw a Little Leaguer being told by his coach, "Hold at third," and his mother yelling, "Johnny, you come home this instant."

An Art Form

Heckling umpires can be an art form. Three favorite put-downs are:

"Hey, ump, if you follow the white line, you'll find first base."

"Hey, ump, how can you sleep with all the lights on?"

"Hey, ump, shake your head—your eyes are stuck."

The Greatest!

A little boy was overheard talking to himself as he strutted through his backyard carrying a ball and bat and shouting, "I'm the greatest hitter in the world!" Then he tossed the ball into the air, swung at it, and missed.

"Strike one!" he yelled. Undaunted, he picked up the ball and repeated, "I'm the greatest hitter in the world!" When it came down, he swung again and missed. "Strike two!" he cried.

The boy paused a moment, examined the ball, spit on his hands, adjusted his hat, and repeated, "I'm the greatest hitter in the world!"

Again he tossed the ball up and swung

at it. He missed. "Strike three!"

"Wow!" he exclaimed. "I'm the greatest *pitcher* in the world!"

Dog-Ball

During a crucial kids' sandlot baseball game, a spectator was surprised to see a dog walk out to the pitcher's mound, wind up, and strike out the other all-star team. Later, he would score two home runs.

"That's incredible," the spectator exclaimed to the man sitting next to him.

"Yes," the man said, "but he's terrible disappointment to his parents. They wanted him to play football."

Good Manners

"Look, Billy," the coach said, "you know the principles of good sportsmanship. You know the Little League doesn't allow temper tantrums, shouting at the umpire, or abusive language."

"Yes sir, I understand."

"Good, Billy. Now, would you please explain that to your mother?"

SWINGERS

He doesn't have a good sense of the strike zone. He once swung at a ball that the pitcher threw to first, trying to pick off a runner.

GOOD NIGHT!

We keep losing games, but our team continues to have a T-shirt night, cap night, a bat night. . . . How about something exciting this season like a "Winning Night?"

WINNING RUN

Coming home from his Little League game, Bud excitedly swung open the front door and hollered, "Anyone home?"

His father immediately asked, "So how did you do, son?"

"You'll never believe it!" Buddy announced. "I was responsible for the winning run!"

"Really? How'd you do that?"

"I dropped the ball."

CONTROL

A rookie pitcher was struggling at the mound, causing the catcher to walk up to have a talk. "I've figured out your problem," he told the young southpaw. "You always lose control at the same point in every game."

"When is that?"

"Right after the National Anthem."

BASEBALL DATE

It was only her second date with a diehard baseball fan, and Judy was a little nervous. It was her fault they arrived at the ball park a full hour after the game had started.

Taking her seat, Judy glanced up at the scoreboard. It was a tight pitcher's battle, bottom of the fifth, 0–0. "Look, Charlie," she exclaimed with relief, "we haven't missed a thing."

LITTLE LEAGUER

"I don't understand you, Skeets," said the Little League coach to one of his slower players. "The distance between first and second base is exactly the same as the distance between second and third. What's your excuse?"

"Gee, coach," answered Skeets, "everyone knows there's a short stop between second and third."

BRUTISH OFFICIATING

A notoriously surly and boorish baseball umpire returns home after a long road trip. He settles back into his easy chair and calls his little boy over to sit on his lap.

"No" says the lad. "The son never sits on the brutish umpire."

THE GOLDEN STATE

"I really like playing ball in San Jose," said the minor league player to his roommate.

"Hank, here in California there are lots of Spanish names," advised the all-knowing roommate. "The natives pronounce the letter 'J' as an 'H.' We say 'San Hosay.'"

"Hmm."

"By the way, when do we play there again?"

"In Hune and Huly."

NEIGHBOR'S WINDOW

A boy's dad scolded him for breaking a neighbor's window with a baseball. "What did he say to you when you broke his window?" asked the father.

"Do you want to hear what he said with or without the bad words?"

"Without, of course."

"Well, then, he said nothing."

Q & A

Q: Why did the baseball player go to jail?
A: Because he was caught trying to steal second base!

Q: Why does it get hot after a baseball game?
A: Because all the fans leave.

Q: Why did the baseball player take his bat to the library?

A: Because his teacher told him to hit the books.

Q: What do you call a baseball with bugs on it?

A: A fly ball.

Q: Why didn't the first baseman get to dance with Cinderella?

A: He missed the ball.

IN TROUBLE

Unable any longer to bear the indifference of Tony, her baseball-crazy husband, Boston native Sophie yelled at him, "You love the Red Sox more than you love me!"

Tony turned around and replied, "I love the *Yankees* more than I love you!"

UMPIRE-ITIS

Fred is a minor-league umpire. He's used to being heckled and bad-mouthed by fans. But he really got a surprise at an exhibition game in Seattle. After a long search for a place to change clothes, Fred finally located a room with a neatly lettered sign: UMPIRES' DRESSING ROOM.

As he was about to go in, however, he inspected the sign more closely. Below the printed ID was the same message—printed in Braille.

YOGI BERRA QUOTES

"Always go to other people's funerals; otherwise they won't come to yours."

"If the people don't want to come out to the ballpark, nobody's gonna stop them."

"No wonder nobody comes here; it's too crowded."

"We make too many wrong mistakes."

KIDS' BASEBALL RIDDLES

Who is Count Dracula's favorite person on the team?

The bat boy.

Where is the largest diamond in the world?

On a baseball field.

What is the best way to get rid of flies?

Sign up some good outfielders.

Why was night baseball started?

Because all bats like to sleep in the daytime.

What team cries when it loses?

A bawl club.

Two baseball teams played a game. One team won, but no man touched base. How could that be?

Both were all-girl teams.

BASKETBALL

Someone has said that basketball is an everyman sport. It has inspired eloquent preachers to proclaim such memorable statements as, "The game of life is much like basketball: some score points, while others just dribble."

HEAVEN BOUND

A star basketball player dies and is in line at the pearly gates. Ahead of him is a talkative guy dressed in sunglasses, a loud shirt, a leather jacket, and jeans. St. Peter addresses the noisy guy, "Who are you?"

The guy replies, "I am Joe Espinosa, taxi driver, of Las Vegas."

St. Peter consults his list. He smiles and says to the taxi driver, "Take this silken robe and golden staff and enter the kingdom of heaven." The taxi driver enters through the gates with his robe and staff; then it's the basketball player's turn.

The basketball player stands erect, all seven feet of him, and announces, "Yo, I'm Joseph Snow, NBA Player of the Year."

St. Peter consults his list. Finally, he says to the athlete, "Take this polyester robe and wooden staff and enter the kingdom of heaven."

"Just a minute," says the basketball star. "That man ahead of me was a taxi driver, and he got a silk robe and a twenty-four-karat gold walking stick. How can this be?"

"Up here, we work by results," advised St. Peter. "There is nothing you did as a basketball player that improved your fellowman."

"But what about that taxi driver?" the athlete interrupted.

"While he was careening in and out of Las Vegas traffic, people were in the backseat praying."

REF RIFFS

The captain of a team says to the ref, "My coach wants to know if there is a penalty for thinking."

The ref says, "No."

The captain says, "Well, my coach thinks you're blind!"

As two NBA basketball referees walked through the countryside, they noticed some tracks. First ref said, "Deer tracks?" Second said, "No, bear tracks." However, the conversation ended abruptly when a train hit them.

FINAL EXAM

Two college basketball players were taking an important exam. If they failed, they'd be on academic probation and not allowed to play in the big game the following week. The exam was fill-in-the-blanks. The last question read, "Old MacDonald had a _____."

Bubba was stumped. He had no idea how to answer, but he knew he needed this answer to play in the big game next week. So he tapped Tiny on the shoulder and asked for the answer to the last question.

Tiny carefully turned around to Bubba and said, "Bubba, you're so stupid. Everyone knows Old MacDonald had a *FARM*."

"Oh yeah," said Bubba. "I remember now." After a long pause, he tapped Tiny on the shoulder and whispered, "Tiny, how do you spell farm?"

"You are really dumb, Bubba. That's so easy. Farm is spelled E-I-E-I-O."

KNOCK, KNOCK

Who's there?
  Tijuana.
Tijuana who?
  Tijuana shoot some hoops later?

PAY OFF

One college hoopster was offered a chance to play in the pros if he'd quit school. He turned down the offer because it would have meant a pay cut.

One college basketball player is making so much money, they plan to give him an unlisted jersey number.

Basketball is supposed to build bodies. Baloney! I watched four games this weekend, and look at my flab.

CLASS

The psychology instructor had just finished a lecture on mental health and was giving an oral test. Speaking specifically about manic depression, she asked, "How would you diagnose a patient who walks back and forth screaming at the top of his lungs one minute, then sits in a chair weeping uncontrollably the next?"

A young man in the rear raised his hand and answered, "A basketball coach."

TRIVIA TRIO

- Basketball got its name from the half-bushel peach baskets used as goals by the game's originator, James A. Naismith, in 1891.
- According to manufacturer Spaulding, the average lifespan of an NBA basketball is ten thousand bounces.
- In 1894, A. G. Spaulding & Bros. of Chicopee, Massachusetts, invented the first official basketball. The first balls were made of panels of leather that were stitched together over a rubber bladder.

TRUE BOBBY KNIGHT STORY

In the 1980 Olympics, the United States basketball team, coached by Bobby Knight, easily beat the Chinese team. When asked about the win, Bobby said, "It was a lot of fun playing the Chinese, but an hour later, we wanted to play them again!"

MAN CALLED "JOE"

A basketball player we'll call "Joe" made a terrible mistake. He robbed a convenience store in his own neighborhood. The owner of the store instantly recognized the 6'7" star hoopster despite his pathetic attempt to wear a mask. When the owner said, "Joe, don't do this, okay?", the familiar masked man replied, "Naw, it ain't me, man. It ain't me."

PUTTING UP WITH JOCKS

The basketball coach stormed into the university president's office and demanded a raise right there and then.

"Please," protested the college president, "you already make more than the entire history department."

"Yeah, maybe so, but you don't know what I have put up with," the coach fumed. "Look."

He went out into the hall and grabbed a jock who was jogging down the hallway. "Run over to my office and see if I'm there," he ordered.

Twenty minutes later, the young man returned, sweaty and out of breath. "You're not there, sir," he reported.

"Oh, I see what you mean," conceded the president, scratching his head. "I would have phoned."

SLOPPY DRIBBLES

Q: How many NCAA basketball players does it take to change a lightbulb?
A: Only one. But he gets money, a car, and three credit hours for doing it.

Q: Why did the chicken cross the basketball court?
A: Because it heard the referee calling fouls.

MISQUOTES

Shaquille O'Neal, on his lack of championships: "I've won at every level except college and pro."

Chuck Nevitt, North Carolina State basketball player, explaining his nervousness to his coach: "My sister's expecting a baby, and I don't know if I'm going to be an uncle or an aunt."

Anonymous basketball coach at Texas A&M, recounting what he told a player who received four Fs and one D: "Son, looks to me like you're spending too much time on one subject."

THE INTERVIEW

"He's really great on the court," a sportswriter said of a college basketball player in an interview with his coach. "But how's his scholastic record?"

"Why, he makes straight A's," replied the coach.

"Wonderful!" said the sportswriter.

"Yes," agreed the coach, "but his B's are a little crooked."

NEVER FAILS

Whenever I go to a ball game, I always end up in the same seat—between the hot dog vendor and his best customer.

Murphy's Laws of Spectator Sports: Exciting plays occur only while you are watching the scoreboard or out buying garlic fries.

ACTUAL HOOPSTER QUOTES

A senior player at the University of Pittsburgh: "I'm going to graduate on time no matter how long it takes."

A coach is reported to have demanded, "You guys line up alphabetically by height," and "You guys pair up in groups of three, and then line up in a circle."

O'Neal on whether he had visited the Parthenon during his visit to Greece: "I can't really remember the names of the clubs that we went to."

A certain Orlando general manager, discussing his team's 7–27 record: "We can't win at home. We can't win on the road. I just can't figure out where else to play."

An anonymous New Orleans general manager, after a loss, was asked what he thought of the refs: "I'm not allowed to comment on lousy officiating."

ONE-LINERS PLUS

Our center's not very bright. I think he's banged his head on too many doorways.

He's such a versatile player he can do anything wrong.

The NBA game is spectacular. You see millionaires running all over the floor. It's like watching the Senate on C-Span.

Our center is a yoga master. He learned yoga attempting to fit into airline seats.

He's the oldest player in the NBA. He leads the league in career sweat.

The coach has a run and shoot offense. If an opponent outruns you, the coach shoots you.

FATHER AND SON

A father and son were watching a basketball game on television. The father was getting more and more upset as a player on the team he supported kept giving away fouls.

"What an idiot," he shouted. "What on earth is he doing playing in such an important game?"

His son sat quietly for a while, then said, "Daddy, maybe it's his ball."

SHORT JUMPS

Which runs longer, the Energizer bunny or the NBA playoffs?

He's so tall he looks like a flagpole with hair. In the off-season he models for silos.

Coach after a big loss: "Their players put their pants on the same as our players do. It just takes us longer to pull them up."

So-and-so is one of the finest officials money can buy.

I would never think of making fun of our point guard's height. I wouldn't stoop so low.

We have so many injuries the team picture is an X-ray.

He's the shortest player in the league—so short he can keep his feet warm just by breathing.

He's so short he fell off the ladder while picking strawberries.

I won't say he's overweight, but his stomach crosses midcourt three steps before he does.

FREE THROWS

I can understand why basketball shorts keep getting longer and longer. If I had knees like some of those guys, I'd want to hide them, too.

It's obvious why losers are not winning. Their shorts are too long and their shots are too wide.

College basketball exists only out of necessity. If there were no basketball, it would be necessary for players to attend class.

I can remember the good old days of basketball—when they shot the ball *up* at the basket, not down into it.

I play in the over-forty basketball league. We don't have jump balls. The ref just puts the ball on the floor, and whoever can bend over and pick it up gets possession.

"March Madness" also describes the mood of anyone working on their income tax forms.

The first rule of watching basketball on TV: Watch only the last two minutes. Nothing much happens until then, and those two minutes will last a half hour.

RANDOM SHOTS

Q: How does Michael Jordan change a
   lightbulb?
A: He holds it in the air, and the world
   revolves around him.

He's so short, he wasn't born and raised; he
was born and lowered.

Our forward was so slow that when it
rained, he rusted.

They're a team in transition. They're going
from bad to worse.

We have so many injuries we're consider-
ing hiring nurses for cheerleaders.

Re: Michael Jordan: "I've guarded guys
who could leap before, but all the others
came down."

Our point guard is so worn down that when
two vultures flew over him the other day,
one looked at the other and said, "We're too
late. Somebody already beat us to him."

KIDS' BASKETBALL RIDDLES

Who was the basketball player's favorite poet?

Longfellow.

What kind of a person plays basketball with a shirt and tie on?

A gym dandy.

What disease makes you a better basketball player?

Athlete's foot.

BOWLING

The wise old man of the alleys had profound revelations about this popular sport. Here is a sample: "If you can't hear a pin drop, there is something definitely wrong with your bowling." Wow. Now that's wise. And another one: "A left-handed dog that bowls should be called a 'southpaw.'"

REALISTIC RULE ADDITIONS

When your team is about ten marks down in the eighth or ninth frame, you can invoke the rule, "First team through bowling wins the game," to allow your team a chance.

After a member of the opposing team bowls four strikes in a row, he/she must bowl the next four frames blindfolded. If he/she continues to strike, his/her shoelaces will be tied together for two frames.

When you leave the tenpin and you know you can't make the spare, another member of your team can invoke the "Designated Bowler" rule.

After you have four splits in one game, you may say "King's-X" and take those four frames over. However, if you split on the second time around, you accept it. After all, "Fair is fair."

VEGGIE BOWL

A bowler whose game has fallen off lately walks into a psychiatrist's office with a cucumber up his nose, a carrot in his left ear, and a banana in his right ear. "What's the matter with me?"

With great insight, the shrink says, "You're not eating properly."

AN OBSERVATION

He was a professional bowler before he became a power basketball forward. You should see his "alley-hoop" play.

TEAM BOWLING

Two bowling teams, one all blond (no prejudice implied) and one all brunette, charter a double-decker bus for a weekend bowling tournament in Atlantic City. The brunette team rides on the bottom of the bus while the blonds perch on the top level.

As the bus weaves through traffic and visits all the sightseeing points, the brunette team below is having a great time. Everyone is whooping it up, when someone suddenly realizes nothing can be heard from the blonds' level. Dashing up the stairs, a brunette from below finds all the blonds sitting frozen with fear, staring straight ahead with white knuckles.

The brunette asks, "What's the trouble up here? We're having a grand time downstairs." One of the blonds from the upstairs team looks up and says, "Well sure, *you* have a driver!"

SHORT TAKES

Bowling is a sport that should be right down your alley.

"Something's wrong with my bowling delivery," Tom said gutterally.

KIDS' BOWLING RIDDLES

What is the quietest sport?
Bowling, because you can hear a pin drop.

Why are good bowlers like a labor union?
Because they strike a lot.

What kind of dog hangs around bowling alleys?
A setter.

Why do good bowlers play so slowly?
Because they have time to spare.

What can you do with old bowling balls?
Give them to elephants for shooting marbles.

BOXING/WRESTLING

There was a time when the sports of the square ring were considered serious manly arts. But today, with choreographed television wrestling and the front-page antics of the likes of Mike Tyson, gentlemanly fisticuffs have become fodder for comedians. The results are such jokes as:

Boxer (or Wrestler, if you prefer): Doc, this ointment you gave me makes my arm smart.
Doc: Then why not rub some on your head?

THE AWFUL TRUTH

"Just think of it," said the braggart boxer to his manager. "Tonight I'll be fighting on television before millions of people."

"Yes," replied the weary manager, "and they'll all know the results of the fight at least ten seconds before you do."

PRO BOXING

One basketball center entered professional boxing after retiring from NBA. He's since developed a cauliflower navel.

THOU SHALT NOT GAMBLE

I once lost a wager on a World Wrestling Federation match. My guy was pinned in ten seconds. I couldn't understand it. He'd won the rehearsal.

I know a fellow who makes only mental bets. The other day he lost his mind.

DRAC'S BOXER

If a boxer was knocked out by Dracula, what would he be? He'd be out for the Count.

TO THE DOGS

Mave: You remind me of my favorite boxer.
Dave: Mike Tyson?
Mave: No, he's called Fido.

CANVAS TALK

Spike: My bro's a boxer.
Ike: Oh yeah? What's his fightin' name?
Spike: Van Gogh, because he's always on
the canvas.

AT THE CORNER

A fighter was taking a terrific beating.
When the bell rang, he staggered to his
corner. Dousing him with a bucket of
water, his manager suggested, "Let him hit
you with his left for a change. Your face is
crooked."

QUICK ROUNDS

He was a crossword-puzzle boxer. He
entered the ring vertical and left horizontal.

When I was a fighter, I kept my head. I
lost my teeth, but I kept my head.

He boxed as Kid Candle. One blow and
he was out.

Written on a boxer's tombstone: "You can stop counting. I'm not getting up."

She was only a prizefighter's daughter, but she certainly knew all the ropes.

MISQUOTES

Boxing promoter Dan Duva on Mike Tyson hooking up again with promoter Don King: "Why would anyone expect him to come out smarter? He went to prison for three years, not Princeton."

A.M. OR P.M.?

His trainer told him to stay down until eight. He looked up from the canvas and asked, "What time is it now?"

WRESTLING FACTS

Wrestlers laugh at petty protective helmets and shin guards.

Wrestler managers get to hit other wrestlers; football managers just get stressed and lose their hair.

Wrestling has good video games. "Super Bass Fishing" was never that great.

Wrestlers tend to brawl all over the arena; football players are penalized for being offside.

Wrestling matches don't stop and start and stop and start and stop and start like football.

Wrestling events aren't delayed by bad weather; Wimbledon lasts double the time with rain.

Wrestling main events don't often turn out to be thirty-second jokes. Boxing should take note.

KIDS' BOXING RIDDLES

When is a man like a dog?
When he is a boxer.

What is the difference between a boxer
and a man with a cold?

*A boxer knows his blows; a man with a
cold blows his nose.*

What is a prizefighter's favorite drink?
Punch.

CRICKET

FOR THE BRITS AMONG US

Those who attempt to equate baseball with cricket are in for a rude awakening. The following is a Yank's fact sheet of British cricket facts.

- There are eleven players on a team.
- All running is between two bases.
- The ball can be hit any direction.
- Each team does all its batting in a single inning.
- A batter can run when he chooses, not every time he hits the ball.
- After one team finishes batting, there is a tea break before the other team gets up to bat.
- A high-scoring game can last seven hours or more.
- In Great Britian, a typical cricket game can last five to six hours; four to five hours of actual play, the rest of the time for lunch, tea, refreshments, and other pauses.

CRICKET FITNESS

Two men were discussing the importance of fitness for the game of cricket. Said the fat one, "When I'm at the crease [home base], my body is highly tuned and taut as a bowstring. The bowler [pitcher] comes up, bowls [pitches], and my brain snaps out a command to my body to get quickly behind the line [batter's box], raise the bat, and execute a perfect stroke [hit]."

"Then what happens?"

"My body says, 'Who, me?' "

SUBJECT: MILLINERY

George: That bowler's just got a hat trick.

Wife: Why is it called a hat trick?

George: Because it's performed by a bowler.

GOTTA BE KIDDIN'

A cricket walked into a London sporting goods store.

"Hey," said the clerk, surprised to see an insect with an interest in sports. "We have a game named after you."

"Really?" asked the cricket modestly.
"You have a game called Jiminy?"

A LIMERICK

A Sussex fast bowler called Lyall,
Took a run-up of nearly a mile.
In one Gillette Cup
He never turned up,
And was last seen just south of the Nile.

WICKET VIEWS

Joe: That was the best inning I ever
played.
Captain: Well, you mustn't let that dis-
courage you.

Phil: You're looking glum.
Bill: Yeah, my doctor says I can't play
cricket.
Phil: Really? I didn't know he'd ever seen
you play!

Tom: The town team wants me to play for
them very badly.
Ron: Well, you're just the man for the job.

THE VICAR'S FIRST GAME

The shy young vicar had been enticed to play on the village team. Although he'd never played before, he gave the first ball a resounding whack and sent it out of the grounds.

"Run," yelled his teammate.

"Don't worry," said the embarrassed minister. "I'll buy you a new ball."

DEVILS VERSUS ANGELS

The Devils challenged the Angels to a game of cricket.

"But we've got all the players," said the Angels.

"Yes, but we've got all the umpires," exclaimed the Devils.

KNOCK, KNOCK

Who's there?
Cricket.
Cricket who?
Cricket neck, man. I can't bend over.

KIDS' CRICKET RIDDLES

What insect loves sports?
A cricket.

Why couldn't Robin play cricket?
He's lost his bat, man.

Which team plays cricket in a three-piece suit?
The Vest Indies.

CYCLING

There are few cycling jokes making the rounds today. Lance Armstrong's multiple wins in the Tour de France, coupled with his great rise over adversity, has shut up the comics who liked to call cyclists "Lycra-clad peddlers who go around in circles."

DOG TRAINING

"I've really had it with my dog. He'll chase anyone on a bicycle."

"So what are you going to do, lock him in the backyard? Sell him?"

"No, nothing that drastic. I think I'll just confiscate his bike."

HOGWASH

I was speeding down a narrow, twisting, mountain road during a training session. A woman was driving very slowly uphill, honking her horn and shouting at me, "Pig! Pig!"

I made an evil face at her and shouted

back, 'Out of my way, you old cow!' Then I collided with the pig."

IN TANDEM

An overzealous traffic cop stopped a country vicar making his rounds on his bicycle. After checking the bike thoroughly and finding nothing, he had to let the cleric go.

You will never arrest me," declared the vicar, "because God is with me wherever I go."

"Well, then," said the cop, "I'm ticketing you for carrying a passenger on a single-seat vehicle."

AUSSIE MOUNTAIN BIKE SLANG

auger (v) To involuntarily take samples of the local geology, usually with one's face, during a crash.

death cookies (n) Fist-sized rocks that knock your bike in every direction but the one in which you want to proceed.

drillium (*n*) Any part with lots of holes drilled in it to make it lighter.

first blood (n) Credit to the first rider in a group who crashes and starts bleeding as a result.

fred (n) (1) A person who spends a lot of money on his bike and clothing but still can't ride. "What a fred—too much Lycra and titanium and not enough skill." (2) Synonym for poser.

gravity check (n) A fall.

gutter bunny (n) A bicycling commuter.

impedimentia (n) All the junk on a bike that impedes performance and looks bad.

JRA (n) Acronym for "Just Riding Along," a phrase universally uttered by people bringing both halves of their frame and the remains of their fork in for warranty replacement.

vultures (n) Spectators who line up at dangerous obstacles in hopes of seeing blood.

weigh-in weenie (n) An MTB owner (not even necessarily a rider) who is more concerned with how many milligrams a certain component saves off the bike's total weight than with how to be a better rider.

EXTREME RIDING

There was this man from Arizona who decided to ride a ten-speed bike from Phoenix to Flagstaff. He got as far as Canyon City before the mountain road became too steep and he could go no farther.

Three hours later, a Corvette finally pulled over, and the driver offered the biker a ride. Of course, the bike wouldn't fit in the car, so the owner of the Corvette found a piece of rope and tied one end to his bumper and the other end to the bike. He told the biker that if he was driving too fast, the biker should honk the bike horn, and he would slow down.

Everything went fine for the first thirty miles. Suddenly another Corvette blew past them. Not to be outdone, the driver pulling the bike took off after the other Corvette. A short distance down the road the Corvettes, both going well over 120, tore through a speed trap.

The officer noted the speeds from his radar gun and radioed to another officer up ahead that he had two Corvettes headed his way speeding over 120 miles per hour. Then he relayed, "And you're not going to believe this, but there's a guy on a ten-speed bike honking to pass."

SILLINESS

Two pieces of black pavement Tarmac are standing chatting at a coffee bar, when in walks a piece of green Tarmac. The piece of green Tarmac demands a grande latte in a menacing manner. He downs the coffee drink, slams his money down on the bar, and walks out.

The waiter turns to the two pieces of black Tarmac and says, "Well, I'm glad he didn't cause any trouble. I've heard he's a bit of a cyclepath."

You Know You're a Cycling Addict If. . .

You buy your crutches instead of renting them.

You refuse to buy a couch for your living room because that stretch of wall space is taken up by your bike.

You empathize with roadkill.

Your kids take a rear derailleur to Show and Tell.

You use wax on your chain, but not on your legs (women). You use wax on your chain *and* your legs (men).

You take your bike along when you go car shopping—just to make sure it'll fit inside.

You can tell your better half, with a straight face, that it's too warm to mow the lawn, and then push off on your bike for a marathon.

You no longer require a hankie to blow your nose.

BIKE CUSTOMS

A cyclist in Europe was stopped by customs. "What's in the bags?" asked the officer, pointing to a load in the bike carryall.

"Sand," said the cyclist.

"Let me take a look," said the cop.

The cyclist did as he was told, emptied the bags, and proved they contained nothing but sand. Then he refilled the bags, loaded them back on the bike, and continued across the border.

A week later, the same thing happened again, and this continued every week for a year, until one day the cyclist with the sandbags failed to appear.

A few months later, the cop saw the cyclist living it up in a downtown supper club. "You sure had us foxed," said the cop. "We knew you were smuggling something across the border." Looking to see if anyone was listening, the cop said, "I won't say a word, but what were you smuggling?"

"Bicycles!"

Gym Cycling

"Lie flat on your backs, class, and circle your feet in the air as if you were riding your bikes," said the gym teacher. "Fred! What are you doing? Move your feet, young man."

"Oh, I'm freewheeling, sir."

Ouch!

Did you hear about the vampire bike that went around biting people's arms off? It was a vicious cycle.

Q & A

Q: Why did the boy take his bike to bed with him?
A: He didn't want to walk in his sleep.

That Hurt!

John was racing around the neighborhood on his new bike and called out to his mother to watch his tricks. "Look, Mom, no hands! Look, Mom, no feet! *Waaah!* Look, Mom, no teeth!"

KIDS' CYCLING RIDDLES

Why can't a bike stand up by itself?
Because it is two-tired [too tired].

When is a bicycle not a bicycle?
When it turns into a driveway.

Why can't an elephant ride a bicycle?
Because he doesn't have a thumb to ring the bell.

What is a ghost-proof bicycle?
One with no spooks.

EXERCISE/HEALTH

The current fitness craze has opened the flood gates for jokesters and stand-up comedians. If the humor target isn't gym bunnies and diet gurus, it's the latest fad exercise equipment or potion advertised on a late-night infomercial. One of the current rotund comedians testified to his comedy club audience, "My idea of exercise is to rip the wrapper off a Twinkie." Read on!

QUICKIES

George's idea of exercise is to sit in the tub, pull the plug, and fight the current.

I have a new incentive to do sit-ups. I put M&Ms between my toes.

The doctor said walking is better than driving. I said, "When was the last time you saw a mailman who looked healthier than a truck driver?"

I enjoy long walks, especially when they're taken by people who annoy me.

I exercise religiously. I do one sit-up, and then I say, "Amen."

Martha says she gets all the exercise she needs just by bending down to pick up those blank subscription cards that fall out of magazines.

Terry bought a rowing machine, but he hasn't used it yet. He can't tear the carton open.

My approach to exercise is casual. I enrolled in a correspondence course at the health spa.

NEED ANSWER

If swimming is so good for your figure, how do you explain whales?

PUPPY LOVE

Ben's dog chewed the tongue on one of her master's brand-new, expensive running shoes. He hoped to save his investment, so he took them to a cobbler shop. Placing the shoes on the counter, Ben told the repairman, "My dog got hold of this."

The cobbler picked up the shoe, looked it over, and placed it back down on the counter.

"Well, what do you recommend?" Ben asked.

The repairman looked at Ben and announced, "Give your dog the other one."

BILLING

A lawyer and his doctor friend were working out at a fitness center.

"I came here to exercise, but people always end up asking me for advice," complained the doctor to the lawyer. "What do you think I ought to do?"

"Simple," suggested the lawyer. "The next time you give them advice, send a bill."

A few days later the doctor received a bill—from the lawyer.

STRENUOUS KIDS

You know it's back-to-school time when all those kids who spent the summer at exclusive camps learning to be rugged and fit are standing on the corner waiting for the school bus to carry them three blocks to school.

NATURAL AEROBICS

These days many people get their exercise by jumping to conclusions, flying off the handle, dodging responsibility, bending the rules, running down everything, circulating rumors, passing the buck, stirring up trouble, shooting the bull, digging up dirt, slinging mud, throwing their weight around, beating the system, pushing their luck, kicking the system, and stooping to less-than-godly behavior.

MORE NATURAL EXERCISES

Beating around the bush, swallowing my pride, making mountains out of molehills, hitting the nail on the head, wading through paperwork, bending over backwards, jumping on the bandwagon, balancing the books, running around in circles, climbing the ladder of success, putting my foot in my mouth, picking up the pieces. Whew! What a workout!

MORE QUICKIES

His idea of vigorous exercise is to lift his feet while his wife is vacuuming.

Big day for me! I'm taking the training wheels off my exercycle.

I met a friend jogging in the park. Well, she was jogging, and I was sitting on a bench.

I owe my athletic physique to my wife and clean living: "Clean the car. . .clean the attic. . .clean the garage."

A man exercises by sucking his stomach in every time he sees a pretty girl.

There's so much traffic in our gym the stationary bikes have rearview mirrors.

JOGGING ROUTE

Lisa had been driving sixteen hours straight and was still at least six hours from her destination. It was about eight in the morning, and Lisa was very tired. After dozing off and nearly crashing into a telephone pole, she decided to pull onto a side road and rest.

She had just dropped off when an old man in a jogging suit knocked on her car window and asked what time it was. Lisa glanced at her watch. "Eight-fifteen," she said through the window. The old man thanked her and jogged off.

A few minutes later, two more male joggers knocked on her window and asked what time it was. Jerking awake, Lisa checked her watch and let the joggers know it was eight-nineteen. "Thanks," they said and took off down the road.

Lisa looked down the road and saw more runners coming her way. Irritated, she got a pen from the glove box and scribbled "I do not know the time" on a piece of paper, stuck it to the window, and settled back to sleep.

Suddenly, she was awakened by

another jogger. She pointed to the sign and shouted, "Can't you read?" To which the jogger replied, "Sure I can, ma'am. I just wanted to let you know it's eight twenty-seven."

ENGLISH EXERCISER

A bodybuilder was boasting about the weight he could lift. "That's nothing," said a scrawny onlooker. "I know a woman who can lift over a thousand pounds."

"Never," said the amazed bodybuilder.

"Oh yes I do," said the little man. "She's the cashier at my bank."

P.E. CLASS EXCUSES

Coach Tom teaches P.E. at Norris Middle School. The following are notes sent by parents as excuses.

- My son Peter is under doctor's care and should not take P.E. today. Please execute him.
- Please excuse Melody from class yesterday. She was sick and I had her shot.

- Dear Coach: Please excuse John from suiting-up on January 28, 29, 30, 31, 32, and also 33.
- Please excuse Roland from P.E. for a few days. Yesterday he fell out of a tree and misplaced his hip.
- John has not been in class because he had two teeth taken out of his face.

TESTIMONIALS

I have discovered that if you are going to try cross-country skiing, it is wise to start with a small country.

I've learned not to jog. It makes the ice cubes jump right out of my glass.

My grandmother started walking five miles a day when she was sixty-five. She is now ninety-seven, and I have no idea where she is.

Helen Hayes was seventy-three when she said, "The hardest years in life are those between ten and seventy."

I know what Victoria's Secret is: Nobody older than thirty can fit into their stuff.

Amazing! I hang something in my closet for awhile, and it shrinks two sizes.

The only exercise I get is jumping to conclusions.

Inside me there's a thin person struggling to get out, but I can usually sedate her with three or four cupcakes.

I don't exercise. If God wanted me to touch my toes, He would have put them higher on my body.

Every time I get the urge to exercise, I lie down until the feeling passes.

FACTS OF LIFE

Chocolate is a vegetable. It is derived from cacao beans. Bean equals vegetable. Sugar is derived from either cane or beets. Both are plants, which places them in the vegetable category. Therefore, chocolate is a vegetable.

The advantage of exercising every day is that you die healthier.

One of life's mysteries is how a two-pound box of candy can make a woman gain five pounds.

The older you get, the tougher it is to lose weight, because by then your body and your fat are really good friends.

My gym teacher told me to touch my toes. I said, "I don't have that kind of relationship with my feet. Can I just wave?"

THE DIET

A terribly overweight young woman was put on a diet by her doctor. "I want you to eat regularly for two days, then skip a day, and repeat this procedure for two weeks. The next time I see you, you'll have lost at least five pounds."

When the woman returns, she's lost nearly twenty pounds. "Why, that's amazing!" the doctor says. "Did you follow my instructions?"

The woman nodded "I'll tell you, though, I thought I was going to drop dead that third day."

"From hunger?" asked the doctor.

"No, from skipping."

Q & A

Q: What has a hundred legs and lives on yogurt?

A: An aerobics class

Q: What is the first thing you lose on a diet?

A: Your patience.

MORE DIET OBSERVATIONS

Diets are for people who are thick and tired of it.

The doctor told me to think thin. I did and lost four inches around my head.

People who write diet books live on the fat of the land.

WEIGHT LIFTING

I don't believe for a second that weight lifting is a sport. They pick up a heavy thing and put it down again. I call that indecision.

JOGGING SHOES

Joe is a middle-aged man who decides to take up jogging. When he goes to the mall to look at shoes, he is overwhelmed by the huge selection. While trying on a basic pair, he notices a minor feature and asks the clerk about it.

"What's this little pocket thing on the side for?

"Oh, that's to carry spare change so you can call your wife to come and pick you up when you've jogged too far."

KIDS' GOOD HEALTH RIDDLES

Why shouldn't you make jokes about a fat person?

Because it's not nice to poke fun at someone else's expanse [expense].

What is the best way to lose weight?
Learn to play the piano, and you can pound away all you want.

If an apple a day keeps the doctor away, what will an onion do?
Keep everyone away.

What is the best exercise for losing weight?
Pushing yourself away from the table.

FISHING

Fish stories are in a class by themselves. The tellers are usually creative anglers who like to brag about the ones that got away or the honest-to-goodness size of the one he caught in a hidden-away stream where there were no witnesses and, as a good steward, he practices catch-and-release.

What he doesn't tell you is that most of his catches are deformed—the head grows too close to the tail.

A Fishy Story

Two avid fishermen go on a fishing vacation. They rent all the equipment: the reels, the rods, the waders, a rowboat, the car, and even a cabin in the woods. They spend a bundle.

The first day they catch nothing. The same thing happens the second day and the third day. This continues until the last day of their vacation, when one of the men catches a fish.

While they're driving home, they're really depressed. One guy turns to the other and moans, "Do you realize that this one lousy fish we caught cost us fifteen hundred dollars?"

The other guy replies, "Wow! Good thing we didn't catch any more!"

Q & A

Q: What do fishermen and hypochondriacs have in common?
A: They don't really have to catch anything to be happy.

Q: Ten fishermen had a great day's catch at a small lake tucked away up country. Who was the saddest fish that evening?
A: The sole survivor.

A GLOSSARY OF FISHING TERMS

catch and release: A conservation activity that usually happens when the local fish and game warden is within eyeshot of your boat.

hook: (1) A curved, pointy device used to catch fish (2) A clever advertisement to entice a fisherman to spend his life savings on a new rod and reel (3) The punch administered by a fisherman's wife after he spends their life savings on a rod and reel (see also Right Hook and Left Hook).

line: Something you give your coworkers when they ask how your fishing went the past weekend.

lure: A device that is only semi-enticing to fish but will drive a fisherman into such a frenzy that he will max out his credit card before exiting the tackle shop.

reel: A rather heavy object that causes a rod to sink quickly when dropped overboard.

rod: A scientifically designed length of fiberglass that prevents a fisherman from getting too close to the fish.

school: A grouping in which fish are taught to avoid $29.99 lures and hold out for cornflakes with peanut butter instead.

tackle: What your fishing partner did to you as you pulled in the catch of the day.

test: (1) The amount of strength a fishing line provides an angler when landing a fighting fish in a specific weight range (2) A measure of your creativity in blaming "that stinkin' line" for once again losing the fish.

LOTSA LUCK

Fishing season hasn't opened, and an angler who doesn't have a license is attempting to lure a trout when a stranger draws near and asks, "Any luck?"

The fisherman boasts, "Any luck? Why, this is a wonderful spot. I took ten out of this stream yesterday."

"Is that so? By the way, do you know who I am?" asks the stranger.

"Nope."

"Well, meet the new game warden."

"Oh," gulped the fisherman. "Well, do you know who I am?"

"Nope."

"Meet the biggest liar in the state!"

ICE FISHING

Georgie went ice fishing, but wasn't having much luck. He saw a guy across the way who was hauling in a bounty of fish. So Georgie went over to the guy and said, "What are you doing to catch all those fish? I'm just a few feet from you and am catching nothing."

The guy answered in a muffled voice, "Ee yer erms orm."

Georgie didn't understand, and the guy tried again, "Ee yer erms orm."

Georgie still couldn't understand him, so the guy repeated, spitting off to the side, "Spfff. . .I said, keep your worms warm!"

TRUTH WILL OUT

Al: I caught a twenty-pound salmon last week.

Sal: Were there any witnesses?

Al: There sure were. If there weren't, it would have been forty pounds.

BRAGGING

A fisherman was bragging about a monster of a fish he caught. A friend broke in and chided, "Yeah, I saw a picture of that fish, and he was all of six inches long."

"Yeah," said the proud fisherman. "But after battling for three hours, a fish can lose a lot of weight."

MINNOW LINES

He caught a muskie that was so big he took a picture of it and the negative weighed five pounds.

The water in that stream is so polluted that if you catch a trout, he thanks you.

A wife went fishing with her husband. After several hours, she remarked, "I haven't had this much fun since the last time I cleaned the oven."

OLE FISHING

Ole was fishing with Sven in a rented boat. They could not catch a thing. Ole said, "Let's go a bit furder downstream."

So they did, and they caught many monstrous fish. They had their limit, so they went home. On the way home, Sven said, "I marked da spot right in da middle of da boat, Ole."

"You silly," said Ole. "How do you know ve vill get da same boat next time?"

MISQUOTE

"I fish, therefore I lie." Anonymous

BROTHER-IN-LAW STORY

My wife's brother is probably one of the most avid fishermen I know. Returning from a day of fishing near the Chesapeake Bay Bridge, I asked him if they were biting. He replied, "Were they? I had to lie down in the boat to bait my hook."

FIGHTING FISHERMAN

Q: If you have two fishermen in a boat slapping at each other with the oars, what is it called?

A: Rowed Rage!

ANY GATORS?

While a tourist was fishing off the Florida coast, his boat capsized. Even though he could swim, he clung to the side of the upturned boat because he was afraid of alligators. Spotting a beachcomber on the shore, he shouted out to him, "Are there any 'gators around here?"

"Nope," the man yelled back. "Ain't been any 'gators 'round these parts for years."

Feeling more at ease, the tourist commenced swimming leisurely toward shore. When he was about halfway there, he shouted out to the beachcomber again. "How'd you get rid of the 'gators?"

"Oh, we didn't do nothing," the beachcomber yelled back. "The sharks ate every last one of them!"

HEAVE-HO!

Gary is a genuine, 100-percent, true sport fisherman. He once said that he caught a great white shark. Since it wasn't on display in his home, Freddie asked what happened to it. Gary sighed, "Well, it was too small to keep, so me and three other guys threw it back in."

RESTRICTED FISHING

A couple was vacationing at a northern fishing resort. Husband Bill liked to fish at the crack of dawn. Angie, his wife, preferred to read. One morning Bill returned after several hours on the lake and decided to take a short nap.

Angie decided to take the boat out. She was not familiar with the lake, but she rowed out to a nice spot and resumed reading her book. In a few minutes the sheriff putted up alongside and greeted her. "Good morning, ma'am. May I ask what you're doing?"

"Why, I'm reading my book, Officer."

"You're in a restricted fishing area."

"But sir, I'm not fishing. Can't you see that?"

"But you have all the equipment, ma'am. I'll have to take you in and write you up."

"If you do that I will charge you with armed harassment."

"I didn't even draw my gun," groused the sheriff.

"Yes, that's true," Angie responded,

pointing to the sheriff's holster. "But you have all the equipment."

Moral: *Never argue with a woman who knows how to read.*

LITTLE KID

A boy sat on the side of the road with his fishing line down in a drain. Feeling sorry for him and wanting to humor him, a lady gave him fifty cents and kindly asked, "How many have you caught?"

"You're the tenth this morning," was the reply.

MEDITATION

Old fishermen never die; they just smell that way and are debaited.

KIDS' FISHING RIDDLES

What is the difference between a fisherman and a lazy student?

One baits his hook; the other hates his book.

What Spanish musical instrument helps you fish?

A cast-a-net [castanet].

What do atomic scientists do when they go on vacation?

They go fission [fishing].

What is the best way to communicate with a fish?

Drop him a line.

What did one fish say to the other fish?

"If you keep your big mouth shut, you won't get caught."

FOOTBALL

Here's a definition of football that doesn't reflect on the cluelessness of women, dumbness of the players, or the blindness of the officials: "Football is a game where twenty-two big, strong players run around like crazy for two hours while fifty-thousand people who really need the exercise sit in the stands and watch them."

NOW THAT'S LOYALTY

Tim was an avid Kansas City Chiefs fan, but he had a really lousy seat location. Spying through his field glasses, he spotted an empty seat on the fifty-yard line and rushed down to try to snag it.

When he got there, Tim asked the man sitting next to it, "Is this seat taken?" The man replied, "This was my wife's seat. Like me, she was a big fan, but she passed away."

Tim replied, "I'm so sorry to hear of your loss. May I ask why you didn't give her ticket to a friend or relative?"

The man replied, "They're all at the funeral."

UNIVERSITY ENTRANCE EXAM FOR FOOTBALL PLAYERS

(Time limit: three weeks)

What language is spoken in France? _____

Give a dissertation on the ancient Babylonian Empire with particular attention to architecture, literature, law, and social conditions.

Or

Give the first name of Pierre Trudeau.

_____

Would you ask William Shakespeare to:
Build a bridge ____
Sail the ocean ____
Lead an army ____
WRITE A PLAY ____

What time is it when the big hand is on the twelve and the little hand is on the five? _____

What religion is the Pope? (Please check only one answer.)

    Jewish ____
    Catholic ____
    Hindu ____
    Agnostic ____

Metric conversion: How many feet is 0.0 meters? _____

How many commandments was Moses given? (approximately) _____

What are people in America's far north called?

    Westerners ____
    Southerners ____
    Northerners ____

Spell:

    Bush _____
    Carter _____
    Clinton _____

Six kings of England have been named George, the last being George the Sixth. Name the previous five.

———————————————————————

Where does rain come from?

Macy's ____

A 7-11 ____

Canada ____

The sky ____

Can you explain Einstein's Theory of Relativity?

Yes ____

No ____

What are coat hangers for?

_____

"The Star Spangled Banner" is the national anthem for what country? _____

Advanced math: If you have three apples, how many do you have? _____

What does NBC (National Broadcasting Corp.) stand for? _____

You must answer three or more questions correctly to qualify.

MISSING FOOTBALL

A man holding a football leaned over his garden gate and shouted to two boys on the other side of the street, "Is this your ball?"

"Did it do any damage, mister?"

"No, it didn't."

"Then it's ours," said the boy.

FIRST TIMERS

Two elderly sisters donated five dollars to a charity and, to their surprise, won tickets to a football game. Since they had never seen a live football game, Madge thought the free tickets would provide some fun for her and her sister.

"I think so, too," said Mabel. "Let's go!"

They soon found themselves high in a noisy stadium overlooking a large grassy expanse. They watched the kickoff and the seemingly endless back and forth struggles that comprised the scoreless first half.

They enjoyed the band music and cheerleader performance that followed.

Then came the second half. When the

teams lined up for the second half kickoff, Madge nudged her sister. "I guess we can go home now, Mabel," she said. "This is where we came in."

HUDDLE TALK

One NFL team has had so many members experience run-ins with the law, they've adopted a new "Honor System": "Yes, your Honor. No, your Honor."

When you see four of their players in a car, who's driving? The police.

WHAT'S IN A NAME?

The coach asked his assistant, "What's that new fullback's name?"

The assistant said, "He's from Thailand. His name is Bandanakadriy-ariki."

The coach said, "I hope he's good. That'll get me even with the newspapers."

MISQUOTES

A running back in New Orleans, anticipating the new season, is quoted as saying, "I want to rush for one thousand or fifteen hundred yards, whichever comes first."

The president of a team comments on one of his highly paid players: "I told him, 'Son, what is it with you? Is it ignorance or apathy?' He said, 'Coach, I don't know, and I don't care!' "

An anonymous University of Houston receiver, on his coach: "He treats us like men; he lets us wear earrings."

TOUGH CALL

It was a particularly tough football game, and nerves were on edge. The home team had been the victims of three or four close calls, and they were now trailing the visitors by a touchdown and a field goal. When the official called yet another close one in the visitors' favor, the home quarterback blew his top.

"How many times can you do this in a single game?" he screamed. "You were wrong on the out-of-bounds. You were wrong on that last first down, and you missed an illegal tackle in the first quarter."

The official just stared.

The quarterback seethed, but he suppressed the language that might get him tossed from the game. "What it comes down to," he bellowed, "is that you stink!"

The official stared a few more seconds. Then he bent down, picked up the ball, paced off fifteen yards, and put the ball down. He turned to face the steaming quarterback. "And how do I smell from over here?" he calmly asked.

WATER BOY

There was a football player who was a bit deficient academically. Finally, the dean told the young man he could play in the big game if he would memorize the formula for water.

The morning of the big day, the dean called the young player into his office and asked him to recite the formula for water. The player grinned and recited, "H I J K L M N O."

PC TEAM NAMES

The Politically Correct National Football League announces its name changes and schedules for the season:

The Washington Native Americans will host the New York Very Tall People on opening day.

Other key games include the Dallas Western-Style Laborers vs. the St. Louis Uninvited Guests; Minnesota Plundering Norsemen vs. the Green Bay Meat Industry Workers.

In week two, there are several key matchups, highlighted by the showdown between the San Francisco Precious Metal Enthusiasts and the New Orleans Good People. Also, the Atlanta Birds of Prey vs. the Philadelphia National Birds of Symbolic Patriotism; the Seattle Birds of Prey vs. the Phoenix Male Finches.

The Monday night game will pit the Miami Pelagic Percoid Food Fishes against the Denver Untamed Beasts of Burden; The Cincinnati Large Bangladeshi Carnivorous Mammals vs. Tampa Bay's West Indies Free Booters; the Detroit Large Carnivorous Cats vs. the Chicago

Security-Traders-in-a-Declining-Market.

Week nine will feature the Indianapolis Young Male Horses vs. New England Zealous Lovers of Country.

NEWS FLASH

A world-class but drooping NFL team that shall remain nameless delayed practice Wednesday for nearly two hours. One of the players, while on his way to the locker room, happened to look down and noticed a suspicious-looking unknown white powdery substance on the practice field. The head coach immediately suspended practice while the FBI was called in to investigate.

After a complete field analysis, the FBI determined that the white substance unrecognized by the players was the goal line. Practice was resumed after FBI special agents decided the team would probably not encounter the substance again.

FAST ONES

Our offensive line was so good that even our backs couldn't get through it.

As John Madden says, "If you see a defensive line with lots of dirt on their backs, they've had a bad day."

One of our linebackers is so huge he should have a license plate instead of a number.

Did you hear about the world's dumbest center? They had to stencil on his pants, "This end up." On his shoes they put T.G.I.F., "Toes Go In First."

I gave up my hope of being a star halfback the second day of practice. One tackle grabbed my left leg, another grabbed my right, and the linebacker looked at me and said, "Make a wish!"

The placekicker missed his attempt at a field goal. He was so angry, he went to kick himself and missed again.

"I know I told you I love you more than football, honey—but that was during the strike."

Football Wedding

Charley and Harley are talking about their boss's upcoming wedding:

Charley: It's ridiculous. He's rich, but he's ninety-three years old, and she's just twenty-six! What kind of a wedding is that?

Harley: Well, we have a name for it in my family.

Charley: What do you call it?

Harley: We call it a football wedding.

Charley: What's a football wedding?

Harley: She's waiting for him to kickoff!

First Timer

Ben took Lisa, his girlfriend, to her first football game. Afterwards, he asked her how she liked the game.

"I liked it, but I couldn't understand why they were killing each other for twenty-five cents," she asked.

"What do you mean?"

"Well, everyone kept yelling, 'Get the quarter back!'"

LOCKER TALKER

A well-known college football coach has been heard admitting, "I give the same half-time speech over and over. It works best when my players are better than the other coach's players."

Football is not a contact sport. It's a collision sport. Dancing is a good example of a contact sport.

FOOTBALL WIVES

Mort is in his usual place at the breakfast table, reading the morning paper. He comes across an article about a beautiful actress who was about to marry a football player known for his lack of general intelligence.

He turns to his wife and blurts, "I'll never understand why the biggest jerks get the most attractive wives."

His wife replies, "Why, thank you, dear!"

Q & A

Q: How many college football players does it take to change a lightbulb?

A: The entire team! And they all get a semester's credit for it.

Q: If you live in Green Bay, Wisconsin, how do you keep bears out of your backyard?

A: Put up goalposts.

MORE FAST ONES

Our players have a lot on the ball. Unfortunately, it's never their hands.

Some chickens were in the yard when a football flew over the fence. A rooster walked by and said, "I'm not complaining, girls, but look at the work they're doing next door!"

I would have played football, but I have an intestinal problem—no guts.

Husband: Hey, Marie, do you have anything you want to say before the football season starts?

Coach Smith retired due to illness and fatigue. The fans were sick and tired of him.

We have so many players on the disabled list the team bus can park in a handi-capped space.

Wife: It's Super Monday. Football season is over!

The only way they can gain yardage is to run their game films backwards.

It was Erma Bombeck who said, "If a man watches three football games in a row, he should be declared legally dead."

IQ

Albert Einstein arrives at a party, intro-duces himself to the first person he sees, and asks, "What is your IQ?" to which the man answers, "241."

"That is wonderful!" responds Einstein. "We will talk about the mysteries of the universe."

Next Einstein introduces himself to a woman and asks, "What is your IQ?"

The lady answers, "144."

"Excellent. We can discuss politics and current events. We will have much to talk about."

Einstein goes to another person and asks, "What is your IQ?" The man answers, "51."

Einstein responds, "How about them Cowboys?"

TURKEY BALL

The pro football team had just finished its daily practice when a large turkey came strutting onto the field. While the players gazed in amazement, the turkey walked up to the head coach and demanded a tryout. Everyone stared in silence as the turkey caught pass after pass and ran through the defensive line.

When the turkey returned to the sidelines, the coach shouted, "You're terrific! Sign up for the season, and I'll see to it that you get a huge signing bonus."

"Forget the bonus," the turkey said.

"All I want to know is, does the season go past Thanksgiving Day?"

How to Annoy Your Man on Super Bowl Sunday

Take the batteries out of all the remote controls.

Show a sudden interest in every aspect of the game. Especially have him define the offside rule many times.

Plug in a boom box and do your Dancerobics routine.

Decide it's time to dust the house, starting with a particularly good dusting of the television set right at kickoff.

Invite your mother over for the game.

Get a *Better Homes and Gardens* magazine, sit in the room, and read extra-good passages aloud.

Invite your friends over for a Pampered Chef party.

It's your night out with the girls; leave the kids home with him!

WHAT'S A FAN?

A football fan is a guy who'll yell at the quarterback for not spotting an open receiver forty-five yards away, then head for the parking lot and not be able to find his own car.

KNOCK, KNOCK

Who's there?
Wilbur Wright.
Wilbur Wright who?
Wilbur Wright back for the second half after these messages.

SPORTS LAWS

Nothing is ever so bad that it can't be made worse by firing the coach.

A free agent is a contradiction in terms.

Whoever thought up "It's only a game" probably just lost one.

It is always unlucky to be behind at the end of the game.

The trouble with being a good sport is that you have to lose to prove it.

ANOTHER CHANCE

A football coach walked into the locker-room before the game, looked over his star player and said, "I'm not supposed to let you play since you failed math, but we need you in there. So what I have to do is ask you a math question, and if you get it right, you can play."

The player agreed, so the coach looked into his eyes intently and said, "Now concentrate hard and tell me the answer to this. What is two plus two?"

The player thought for a moment and then answered, "Four."

"Did you say four?" the coach asked,

excited that he got it right.

Suddenly all the other players began yelling, "Come on, coach, give him another chance!"

Animal Super Bowl

During a recent Super Bowl, there was another football game of note between big animals and small animals. The big animals were crushing the small animals. At half-time the coach made an impassioned speech to rally the little animals.

At the start of the second half, the big animals had the ball. On the first play, an elephant got stopped for no gain. On the second play, the rhino was stopped for no gain. On the third down, the hippo was thrown for a five-yard loss.

The defense huddled around the coach, who asked excitedly, "Who stopped the elephant?"

"I did," said the centipede.

"Who stopped the rhino?"

"Uh, that was me, too," said the centipede.

"And how about the hippo? Who hit

him for a five-yard loss?"

"Well, that was me as well," said the centipede.

"So where were you during the first half?" demanded the coach.

"Well," said the centipede, "I was having my ankles taped."

TRAGEDY REPORT

The University of Florida football coach told Gator fans that a fire at Auburn's football dorm had destroyed twenty books: "But the real tragedy was that fifteen hadn't been colored yet."

KIDS' FOOTBALL RIDDLES

Why is an airline pilot like a football player?
They both want to make safe touchdowns.

What color is a cheerleader?
Yeller [yellow].

What did the football say to the football player?
"I get a kick out of you."

GOLF

Of all the sport joke categories, none are as full of laughs as golf. There are all the Bob Hope remarks, "Golf is *flog* spelled backwards," "This morning I missed a hole in one by eight strokes," and "With the price of golf gear today, it's not only the clubs that get the shaft!"

Not to mention a well-known television evangelist, "Isn't Joe out of the bunker yet? How many strokes has he had?"

"Fifteen club and one apoplectic." And so it goes. Here are some more.

TROUBLE

On the seventh tee Tom sliced his shot deep into a wooded ravine. Taking his eight iron, he clambered down the embankment in search of his lost ball.

After many minutes of hacking at the underbrush, he spotted something glistening in the foliage. As he drew nearer, he discovered it was an eight iron in the hand of a skeleton.

Tom called up to his friend. "Pete, I've

got trouble down here."

"What's the matter?" Pete called down.

"Bring me my wedge," Tom shouted. "You can't get out of here with an eight iron."

CADDY TROUBLE

Golfer: Notice any improvement since last year?

Caddy: Polished your clubs, didn't you?

Golfer: Why do you keep looking at your watch?

Caddy: This isn't a watch, sir. It's a compass.

Golfer: Caddy, why didn't you see where that ball went?

Caddy: Well, it doesn't usually go anywhere, Mr. Norris. You caught me off guard.

THE FOURSOME

Four men were playing a round of golf. "These hills are getting steeper as the years go by," one complained.

"The sand traps seem to be bigger than I remember them, too," said another senior.

After hearing enough, the oldest and wisest of the four, at eighty-seven, said, "Just be thankful we're still on the right side of the grass!"

NEWBIE

When Mr. McKenna retired, his coworkers gave him a good-bye gift set of golf clubs. After looking at them for a few weeks, he finally decided he'd try the game. He asked the local pro for lessons, explaining that he knew nothing about the game.

The pro showed him the stance and swing, then said, "Just hit the ball toward the flag on the first green."

Novice McKenna teed up and smacked the ball straight down the fairway and onto the green, where it stopped inches from the hole.

"Now what?" McKenna asked the speechless pro.

"Uh, you're supposed to hit the ball into the cup," the pro finally said, after he was able to speak again.

"Oh, great! Now you tell me," said the beginner disgustedly.

WOMEN'S TEE

As Joe started to eye up his golf ball, hoping that it would fly beyond all previous driving hits, a voice came behind him said, "Hey buddy! Don't you know you're hitting from the women's tee?"

Joe smugly looked at the avid golf pro/lawyer and said, "Hey buddy, don't you know this is my second shot?"

EXPECTANT GOLF

The Lamaze class was going full swing with a room full of pregnant women and their husbands. Breathing and exercise were the evening topics. "Ladies, walking is especially beneficial for you. And, gentlemen, it wouldn't hurt you to go walking with your wives."

The room got quiet, then a man shot up his hand and asked, "Is it all right if she carries a golf bag while we walk?"

THE SILENT GOLFER

A man was just about to tee off when he felt a tap on his shoulder; a man handed him a card that read, "I am a deaf mute. May I play through, please?"

The first man angrily gave the card back and communicated, "No, you may not play through!" He then whacked the ball onto the green and left to finish the hole.

Just as he was about to sink the ball into the hole, he was hit on the head with a golf ball, laying him out cold.

When he came to a few minutes later, he looked around and saw the deaf mute sternly looking at him, one hand on his hip, the other holding up four fingers.

QUIT PLAYING WHEN. . .

You have had three putts and your group members tell you that you're still away.

You can remember for a week the one good shot you had in the round.

The ball retriever is the most used piece of equipment in your bag.

You and your group have rules for mulligans.

You leave the pin in when you are on the fringe eight feet away in the hope it will stop your ball.

The starter leaves a one-hour gap after your tee-off time.

You have more than the regulation fourteen clubs in your bag, including three putters.

When you call fore on a par three and everyone runs to the green for safety.

The club has named a pond in front of the green after you.

No Kiddin'?

Harry: You know what your main golf problem is?

Terry: What?

Harry: You stand too close to the ball after you've hit it.

A POEM

I think that I shall never see
A hazard rougher than a tree;
A tree o'er which my ball must fly
If on the green it is to lie.

A tree which stands that green to
    guard,
And makes the shot extremely hard;
A tree whose leafy arms extend
To kill the six iron shot I send.

A tree that stands in silence there,
While angry golfers rave and swear.
Irons were made for fools like me
Who cannot ever miss a tree.

—AUTHOR UNKNOWN

YUCK, YUCK

Q: Why do golfers wear two pairs of
    pants?
A: In case they get a hole in one.

GOLF BUSINESS

Jason, looking depressed, says to his business partner, "My doctor tells me I can't play golf."

"So he's played with you, too."

Golf is a lot like business. You drive hard to get in the green and then wind up in the hole.

The late Joe E. Lewis used to say, "I play in the low eighties. If it's any hotter than that, I won't play."

TEE FOR TWO

Teddy is the picture of a golf style, but on the course he is something else. He slices his first drive deep into the woods. Rather than accept a penalty, he decides to try using an iron to get back onto the fairway. His ball ricochets off a tree and strikes him in the forehead, killing him.

When he arrives at the Pearly Gates, St. Peter greets him. "You look like a golfer. Are you any good?"

Teddy replies, "Absolutely! I got here in two, didn't I?"

HEAVENLY GOLF

Toward the end of a particularly trying round of golf, Troy was the picture of frustration. He'd hit too many fat shots. Finally he blurts out to his caddie, "I'd move heaven and earth to break a hundred on this course."

Try heaven," replied the caddie. "You've already moved most of the earth."

OUT GOLFING

Two not-too-brilliant rustics are out golfing and are stuck on the sixteenth green when a foursome comes to play through. One guy asks, "What seems to be the trouble?"

The first rustic answers, "We both hit to the green and when we got here, one ball was in the cup and one was balanced on the edge of the cup. We both shoot Titleist #3 balls, so we can't figure out who got the hole in one."

The other golfer looks at the two balls and replies, "Which one of you was playing with the orange ball?"

PARADISE GREEN

A husband and wife driving home one night ran into a bridge abutment. Both were killed. They arrived in heaven and found it had a magnificent golf course. With a giggle, the husband asked, "You want to play a round?"

"Sure!" she said. So they teed off on the first hole. Suddenly Wife noted a troubled look cross Husband's face. "What's wrong?" she asked.

Husband answered, "This place is fabulous. If it hadn't been for your stupid oat bran, we could have been here years ago."

WELL, SONNY. . .

Young Alfie was an avid golfer, so one afternoon when he found himself with a few hours to spare, he decided to get in nine holes before he had to head home.

Just as Alfie was about to tee off, an

old gentleman walked onto the tee and asked if he could play along with him for a twosome. "I suppose so," Alfie responded.

To his surprise, the old man played fairly quickly. He didn't hit the ball too far, but he plodded along consistently and didn't waste any time.

Finally, they reached the ninth fairway, and Alfie found himself with a tough shot. There was a large pine tree right in front of his ball and directly between his ball and the green.

After several minutes of watching Alfie debate how to hit the shot, the old man finally said, "You know, when I was your age, I'd hit the ball right over that tree."

With that challenge before him, Alfie swung hard and hit the ball right smack into the top of the tree. It dropped back to the ground not a foot from where it originally lay.

"Of course," the old man commented, "when I was your age, that pine tree was only six feet tall."

GOLF GUN

Two New York City detectives were investigating the murder of one Juan Flores.

"How was he killed?" asked one detective.

"With a golf gun," the other replied.

"A golf gun? What is a golf gun?"

"I don't know, but it sure made a hole in Juan!"

SHORT PUTTS

There are thousands of people who are worse golfers than he is. Of course, they don't play.

A Scotsman gave up the game after twenty-five years. He lost his ball.

I'm not saying his game is bad, but if he grew tomatoes, they'd come up sliced.

One of the quickest ways to meet new people is to pick up the wrong ball.

He cut ten strokes off his score. He stopped playing the last hole.

Eddie: What do you think of my game?
Caddie: It's okay, but I like golf better.

Golf Pro: Are you two ladies here to learn
to play golf?
Lady One: My friend is. I learned yesterday.

Wife: You're so involved with golf that
you can't remember the day we were
married.
Husband: That's what you think. It was the
same day I sank a thirty-five-foot putt.

ANONYMOUS CONFESSION

"I don't play golf. Personally, I think there's
something psychologically wrong with any
game in which the person who gets to hit
the ball the most is the loser."

COINCIDENCE

"You must be the worst caddie in the world,"
said the dejected golfer after a disastrous
afternoon on the course.

"I doubt it, sir," replied the caddie.
"That would be too much of a coincidence."

Down and Out

A hacker golfer spends the day on the golf course of an uppity country club, playing golf and enjoying the benefits of a complimentary caddy. Being the hacker that he is, he plays poorly all day. Somewhere near the eighteenth hole, he spots a lake off to the right of the fairway. In desperation, he moans to his caddy, "I've played so poorly all day, I think I'm going to drown myself in that lake."

Looking back at him, the caddy responds, "I don't think you could keep your head down that long."

It's Civilization

In less civilized countries, when native tribes beat the ground with clubs and yell, it's called witchcraft. Today, in civilized society, it's called golf.

A Substitution

Official: Too bad, sir, we have no open
    time on the course today.
Golfer: Hey, just a minute—what if

Arnold Palmer and Tiger Woods showed up? I bet you'd have a starting time for them. Right?

Official: Of course.

Golfer: Well, I happen to know neither will be here today, so we'll take their time.

SOME MORE SHORT PUTTS

She: Let me get this straight. The less I hit the ball, the better I am doing.

He: That's right.

She: Then why hit it at all?

As the man said, "I know I can play better than this. I just never have."

In golf, you drive for show and putt for dough.

Golf is a game where the ball lies poorly and the players well.

Real golfers don't cry when they line up their fourth putt.

Golf is an easy game—it's just hard to play.

BAH!

The club grouch was unhappy about everything: the food, the assessments, the parking, the other members. The first time he hit a hole in one he complained, "Just when I needed the putting practice!"

HOPE WORKS

It was the inimitable Bob Hope who said, "If you watch a game, it's fun. If you play it, it's recreation. If you work at it, it's golf."

WONDER WOODS

Stevie Wonder and Tiger Woods are in a conversation when Woods turns to Wonder and asks, "How is the singing career going?"

Stevie Wonder replies, "Not too bad! How's the golf?"

Tiger responds, "Not too bad. I've had some problems with my swing, but I think I've solved that problem."

Wonder suggests, "I've always found

that when my swing goes wrong, I need to stop playing for awhile and not think about it. Then, the next time I play, it seems to be all right."

Surprised, Tiger asks, "You play golf, Stevie?"

Stevie Wonder answers, "Oh, yes. I've been playing for years"

Tiger exclaims, "But you're blind. How can you play golf?"

Wonder replies, "I get my caddy to stand in the middle of the fairway and call to me. I listen for the sound of his voice and play the ball toward him. Then, when I get to the ball, the caddy moves to the green or farther down the fairway, and again I play the ball towards his voice."

"But how do you putt?"

"Well," says Stevie, "I get my caddy to lean down in front of the hole and call to me with his head on the ground, and I just play the ball towards his voice."

Tiger asks, "What's your handicap?"

Stevie answers, "I'm a scratch golfer."

An incredulous Tiger Woods says, "We've got to play a round sometime," and

Wonder replies, "Well, people don't take me seriously, so I can only play for serious money, never less than ten thousand dollars a hole."

Woods thinks about it and says, "Okay, I'm game for that. When would you like to play?"

To which Stevie responds, "Pick a night!"

Kids' Golf Riddles

What did the dentist say to the golfer?
"You have a hole in one."

Where do golfers dance?
At the golf ball.

HIKING/CAMPING/
THE GREAT OUTDOORS

The Good Book tells us that "In the beginning God created the earth." Of course that includes the Grand Canyon, the Smoky Mountains, the Mississippi River, autumn color in New England, Niagara Falls, and all the breathtaking natural sites around the world. What Genesis doesn't go into detail about are other things He created, like poison ivy, gnats, pebbles in hiking shoes, rain that wets matches, nettles, and creepy crawly things that get into sleeping bags.

Hiking and the Law

A lawyer invites his cousin from the Czech Republic to come to America and go hiking with him. The Czech cousin arrives, and very soon they're deep in a forested wilderness. In no time at all, a huge grizzly bear sniffs them out, grabs the Czech cousin, and eats him.

The lawyer runs to the nearest town and tells everyone what has happened. The townsfolk form a search party and return to the forest, where they come across some bears. The town's mayor asks the lawyer to identify the animal that killed his cousin.

"It's that male bear over there."

They kill the bear and rip open his stomach, but find nothing. Then they decide to kill the female bear standing nearby. When they cut her open, they find the poor Czech cousin.

So it all goes to show: "Never trust a lawyer when he says the Czech is in the male."

MISSING MILKY WAY

Sherlock Holmes and Dr. Watson were on a camping and hiking trip. The first night out they had gone to bed and were lying looking up at the sky. "Watson," Holmes said, "look up. What do you see?"

"Well, I see thousands of stars."

"And what does that mean to you?"

"Well, I guess it means we will have another nice day tomorrow. What does that mean to you, Holmes?"

"To me, it means someone has stolen our tent."

ANOTHER BEAR

Two backpackers see a bear about to charge them. One of the hikers takes off his boots and puts on running shoes. His companion says, "You'll never outrun the bear—why are you putting those shoes on?" The guy with the running shoes responds, "I don't have to outrun the bear. I just have to outrun you."

PRACTICAL CAMPING HINTS

When using a public campground, a tuba placed on your picnic table will keep the sites on either side of you vacant.

When smoking fish, never inhale.

You'll never be lost if you remember that moss always grows on the north side of your compass.

You can duplicate the warmth of a down-filled sleeping bag by climbing into a plastic garbage bag with several geese.

Turn old socks into high-fiber beef jerky by smoking them over an open fire.

When camping, always wear a long-sleeved shirt. It gives you something to wipe your nose on.

A hot rock placed in your sleeping bag will keep your feet warm. A hot enchilada works almost as well, but the cheese sticks between your toes.

OLE ON THE TRAIL

Ole is hiking in the mountains of Norway when he slips on a wet rock and falls over the edge of a five hundred foot cliff. He falls twenty feet and grabs hold of a bush that's growing out of a rock. There he hangs over a deep fjord. As his hands get sweaty and he starts losing his grip, he yells out, "Is anybody up there?"

He hears a deep voice ring out. "I'm here, Ole. It's the Lord. Have faith. Let go of that bush, and I will save you."

Ole looks down, looks up, and sobs, "Is anyone else up there?"

KNOCK, KNOCK

Who's there?
Saul.
Saul who?
Saul there is, ain't no more.

RELAXING WEEKENDS

Getting away from their high-stress jobs, May and Trey spend relaxing weekends in their motor home. When they found their peace and quiet disturbed by well-meaning but unwelcome visits from other campers, they devised a plan to assure their privacy.

Now when they set up camp, they place this sign on their RV door: "Insurance agent. Ask about our term-life package."

FURTHER TIPS FOR CAMPERS

Get even with the bear who raided your food container by kicking his favorite stump apart and eating all the ants.

In emergency situations, you can survive in the wilderness by shooting small game with a slingshot made from the elastic waistband of your underwear.

A two-man pup tent does not include two men or a pup.

A potato baked in the coals for one hour makes an excellent side dish. A potato baked in the coals for three hours makes an excellent hockey puck.

KIDS' HIKING RIDDLES

What is the first thing you put on a trail?
Your feet.

What wears shoes but has no feet?
The sidewalk.

Why do you always start a hike with the right foot first?
Because when you move one foot, the other one is always left.

What has a foot on each side and one in the middle?
A yardstick.

HOCKEY

In all probability, dentist readers will turn to this section first. Why? The classic observation about hockey goalies is the plugged gaps in their smiles. A dentist was recently heard complimenting a goalie on his nice, even teeth: one, three, five, seven, nine, and eleven were missing.

MORE TEETH

Hockey players have been complaining about violence for years. It's just that without their teeth, no one can understand them.

They say there are three ways to play hockey: rough, rougher, and "I'll help you find your teeth if you'll help me look for mine."

HOWLER

Our home team wasn't doing very well. During a typically horrible game, none of the players had even taken a shot at the goal. Finally, one got the puck, and a voice from the stands yelled, "Shoot it! The wind's with you!"

FIRST PERSON SINGULAR

I think hockey is a great game. Of course, I have a son who's a dentist.

I knew it was going to be a wild game when a fight broke out in the middle of the National Anthem.

INJURIOUS HOCKEY

Andy came to work limping like crazy. One of his coworkers noticed and asked Andy what happened.

"Oh, nothing," Andy replied. "It's just an old hockey injury that acts up once in a while."

"Gee, I never knew you played hockey," the coworker responded.

"No, I don't," explained Andy. "I hurt it last year when some stupid official put my favorite player in the penalty box. I put my foot through the television screen."

You May Be a Hockey Nut If. . .

You think there are three periods in basketball.

In church when the minister talks about "The Almighty," you look around to see if Wayne Gretsky has come in.

You stand up during a game and hope the puck hits you.

You have your own PowerAde water bottle, and when you squirt water into your mouth, you have to keep yourself from spitting it back out.

You immediately ask "Who won the fight?" when someone says he dropped his gloves.

You add the names of hockey players during your "God blesses" in your prayers.

BUMPER STICKER

Be Kind to Animals. Hug a Hockey
Player.

Q & A

Q: What is a hockey puck?
A: It's a hard rubber disc that players hit
when they are not hitting each other.

Q: How can hockey be revolutionized?
A: Invent a clear Lucite puck.

Q: What's the difference between a hockey
game and a prize fight?
A: In a hockey game, the fights are real.

Q: Did you hear what happened to the
Lake Woebegon ice hockey team?
A: They drowned during spring training.

COOL WAYS TO USE A ZAMBONI

- Get a couple of them and drag
race.
- Do donuts at the face-off
circles.

- Chase squirrels around the parking lot.
- Scare the ice-level broadcasters.
- Do Jeff Gordon impressions.
- Smooth off the ice on your driveway.
- Teach your teenager to parallel park.

HONESTLY

When I was a kid, I thought that hockey players were sent to the penalty box to put in a time-out until their fathers came home from work. Come to think of it, that isn't such a bad idea.

ADVANTAGES OF BEING A GOALIE

- You automatically have a Halloween costume.
- Padding gives the impression that you're really buffed.
- Helmet allows you to double as Darth Vader in any upcoming "Star Wars" prequel/sequel.

- Bruises can really bring out the color of your eyes.

PET PEEVES OF GOALTENDERS

- Players at parties who want to turn a mask upside down for bean dip.
- Pads give the appearance of a fat rear end.
- Frostbite caused by leg splint.
- Fans who throw Hostess Ding Dongs at the net.

THE GOALTENDER'S PSALM

The puck is my shepherd;
I shall not ice.
It maketh me save in unnatural
    positions;
It leadeth me into leg splits;
It restoreth my fan's faith;

It leadeth me in the paths of odd-man
    rushes.
Yea, though I skate in the valley of the
    shadow of the net,

I will fear no sniper;
For my stick is with me;
My facemask and pads they comfort
    me;
they annointeth my body with
    SportsCreme;
My back-up tippeth over!
Surely coaches and trainers shall follow
    me all the games of my life.
And I shall dwell in the ice house
    forever.

KIDS' HOCKEY RIDDLES

What is ice?
    Skid stuff.

When a girl hockey player falls on the ice,
why can't her brother help her up?
    He can't be a brother and assist her [a sister] too.

HORSEMANSHIP

Horse names: Who are these fabled horses? Silver, Scout, Seabiscuit, Trigger, Man-of-War, Black Beauty, Flicka, Secretariat, Black Stallion, Ol' Dobbin, Mr. Ed, Goofy. . .

("He is a horse, isn't he?"

"No, he's a dog. Clarabelle is the horse."

"Clarabelle was a clown on the 'Howdy Doody Show.' "

"She was also a horse in early Disney cartoons."

"She was also my aunt from St. Paul."

"Does that make her a horse?"

"I never said. . .oh, forget it!")

Okay, we will.

BROOKLYN DODGERS

Years ago, when the Dodgers were still in Brooklyn and Leo Durocher was the team's manager, a horse wandered up to the great manager and said, "Why don't you use me on your team, Leo? I can hit and field as well as anyone on your team."

"Get lost," Durocher yelled. "I've got enough troubles."

"Come on, Leo, give me a chance. Try me in the field."

"Okay, just for laughs."

The horse went out into the field and made one spectacular stop after another.

"Amazing," said Durocher. "Come on in and bat."

The horse hit one ball after another over the fence, and Durocher signed the horse on the spot.

Next day, the Dodgers were playing the Giants. The horse repeated his phenomenal fielding and batting. In the sixth inning, the horse was up to bat. The bases were loaded, and he hit one over the Ebbets Field wall.

"Run, run!" Durocher yelled, but the horse just stood there.

"Are you kidding?" said the horse. "If I could run, I'd be racing at Churchill Downs."

Following

Terry and Gus are at the office water cooler, talking about horse racing. Terry is going on and on about how he understands the sport and always wins at the track. When he finally gets around to asking Gus what happens to the horses he follows, Gus says, "The horses I follow usually end up following the other horses."

HORSE TALK

Two horses are talking in the corral. One says, "What kind of saddles do they put on you?"

The other says, "I don't know. What kinds are there?"

"There's English and there's Western."

"Is there a difference?"

"The English doesn't have a horn."

"I guess that must be the one, because I never go out in traffic."

LET THERE BE HORSES

A little boy of six, visiting the country for the first time, came running to his mother. Bubbling over with excitement, he said, "Mama, I just saw a man who makes horses."

"Are you certain?"

"Yup. The horse was almost done. The man was just nailing on his back feet."

"THERE'S A HORSE IN THE TUB"

Joe was trying to lead a horse in the street but was having much trouble. A passerby stopped and asked if he could help. Joe was grateful. After much pushing and shoving, they finally got the animal to the front door of Joe's apartment building. Joe indicated that the horse was to go through the door. More pushing and shoving. Once inside, Joe and the passerby managed to work the horse up the steps and into Joe's apartment on the third floor, then through the living room and into the bathroom, where the horse was deposited into the bathtub.

Wiping the sweat from his brow, the good Samaritan said, "I don't want to be nosy, but this is most unusual."

Joe said, "When my wife comes home she'll look in the bathroom and say, 'There's a horse in there.' How many times in my life will I get the chance to say, 'I know! I know!' "?

You Are a True Horsewoman If. . .

You're willing to use your horse's mane/tail comb to put up your hair.

You use your horse's braiding bands for your own hair.

You give your horse more baths than you get yourself.

You clip your horse more often than you shave your legs.

You don't have air conditioning, but you have two fans in your horse's stall.

You spend more money on your horse's front shoes than you do on all your shoes put together.

Overheard at the Races

I always choose a horse that has excellent breeding. After he leaves the starting gate, he turns around to close it behind him.

His horse came in so late the jockey was wearing pajamas.

Horse sense: that innate sense that keeps horses from betting on people.

If Paul Revere had ridden my horse, we'd still be under British rule.

My horse was right up there with the winning horse when the race started.

TEN HORSES
MOST UNLIKELY TO WIN

1. Future Glue
2. Senor Sleepy
3. Parts on Order
4. Tax Write-Off
5. Two Fat Guys in a Horse Costume
6. Pothole Dancer
7. Two-Legged Pierre
8. Ebola
9. Kevorkian's Delight
10. Gelatina

HUSBANDS VERSUS HORSES

Husbands are less expensive to shoe.

Feeding a husband doesn't require anything that even mildly compares with the hassle of filling a horse up with hay.

If they're playing hard to catch, you may be able to run the man down on foot.

A lame husband can still work.

A husband with a bellyache doesn't have to be walked.

THE HORSE'S ADVANTAGE

If your horse doesn't work out, you can sell him.

Horses don't come with in-laws.

You don't have to worry about your children looking like them.

You never have to iron their saddle pads.

They smell good when they sweat.

They don't want their turn at the computer.

They turn white with age, but not bald.

They don't care what you look like, as long as you have a carrot.

KIDS' HORSE RIDDLES

Which has more legs, a horse or no horse?
   No horse. A horse has four legs, but no horse has six legs.

How can you make a slow horse fast?
   Don't give him any food.

What has two arms, two wings, two tails, three heads, three bodies, and eight legs?
   A man on a horse holding a chicken.

What has six legs but walks with only four?
   A horse with a rider.

HUNTING

One of the great mysteries of the sports world is why ducks have all the glory. Have you ever seen an organization called Crappies Unlimited? Partridges Unlimited? Or even Bambi's Mother Unlimited? No, it's always a duck—a nasty, quacking duck—who annoys us through all those insurance commercials.

In Kansas City there's an upscale restaurant named after them (The Peppercorn Duck Club), khaki trousers carry their likeness (Duck Head), and an certain adult beverage has the species on its label (Cold Duck).

So, next time you see that Ducks Unlimited sticker on the back window of someone's pickup, thank the good Lord that the hunting world isn't attempting to save the aardvark or the common ant. Besides, can you imagine a trophy ant over someone's fireplace?

DUCK HUNTERS

Phil and Gil were duck hunting. For five hours, they had been unable to bag anything. Finally, one turned to the other and suggested, "Maybe we ought to try throwing the dogs a little bit higher."

An Unbearable Situation

A greenhorn was telling his buddy what a great hunter he was. When they arrived at their cabin, the greenhorn suggested, "You get the fire started, and I'll go shoot us something for supper."

In a few minutes, the greenhorn met a grizzly bear. He dropped his gun and took off for the cabin, with the bear in hot pursuit. When he was a few feet away from the cabin, the greenhorn tripped over a log. The bear couldn't stop and skidded through the open cabin door.

The greenhorn got up, slammed the door, and yelled to his friend inside, "You skin that one, and I'll go get us another one."

End of the Season

The Wednesday night church service happened to fall on the last day of hunting season. When the pastor asked his congregation if anyone had bagged a deer this year, not a hand was raised.

Puzzled, the pastor said, "I don't understand. Many of you wives said your husbands were missing last Sunday because of hunting. So to help in your hunting quest, I asked the congregation to pray for your deer and safety."

"It sure worked," groaned one hunter. "They're all safe."

MISQUOTE

It was Johnny Carson who said, "If God didn't want man to hunt, he wouldn't have given us plaid shirts."

ANOTHER SVEN AND OLE STORY

The county game warden died, and Sven and Ole devised a plan that they hoped would land one of them in the position. They flipped a coin, and Ole called it. "You'll be callin' the mayor, Sven," his buddy announced.

So Sven called the mayor and said, "Mr. Mayor, I hear the game warden died last night. If it's all right with you, I'd like to take his place."

With great surprise the mayor replied, "It's all right with me if it's all right with the undertaker."

DEAD DUCK

Three men go duck hunting one day. Two of them are inundated with stories from the third about his "great" duck hunting prowess. After a few hours, each of the first two men have bagged a couple of ducks, but the braggart hasn't taken a shot. They question him about this, so he agrees to show his shooting abilities at the next opportunity.

A few moments later, one lone duck comes flying by. As promised, the boaster stands up and squeezes out one shot. The duck keeps flying.

"Gentlemen, you have just witnessed a miracle," says the braggart, pointing at the receding bird, "for there flies a dead duck!"

THE PESSIMIST

An avid duck hunter was on the lookout for a new bird dog. His search ended when he found a dog that could walk on water to retrieve a duck. Shocked by his find, he was sure none of his friends would believe it.

The first time he took the dog out, he took along a friend who was an avid pessimist. As they waited by the lakeshore, a flock of ducks flew by. They fired, and a duck fell into the lake. The dog responded like a flash and jumped onto the water. Sure as anything, the hound did not sink but instead walked across the water to retrieve the bird, never getting more than his paws wet.

The friend saw everything but didn't say a word.

On the drive home the hunter asked his friend, "Did you notice anything unusual about my new dog?"

"I sure did," responded his friend. "He can't swim."

TIGER QUESTION

A father takes his boy tiger hunting. They're creeping through the underbrush, and the dad says, "Son, this hunt marks your passage into manhood. Do you have any questions?"

"Yes, Dad. If the tiger kills you, how do I get home?"

THREE SHOTS

Two hunting aficionados are out hunting. They decide to separate in order to have a better chance of catching something.

The first hunter says, "If you get lost, fire three shots into the air every hour. That way I can pinpoint you and find you."

After three hours, the second hunter finds he's really lost. He decides to fire three shots into the air as his friend told him. He then waits another hour and does it again. He repeats this until he's out of ammo.

The next morning, the first hunter finds the second hunter with the help of forest rangers.

The first hunter asks, "Did you do what I told you to do if you got lost?"

His friend answers, "I fired three shots into the air every hour on the hour until I ran out of arrows."

TRACKING

Three hunters were stranded in the mountains, and they didn't think they'd be able to get back to civilization for three days. So they all made a plan that each night one would get the food. The first night, the first guy went out and came back with a big deer, causing the man who was to go out the next night to secure food to ask for advice. The successful first hunter admitted to the next hunter that he scored by finding tracks, following tracks, and *bam!* then shooting the deer. The next night, the second hunter went out and scored.

The third guy went out to get a deer and came back hours later, all bloody. The other two hunters asked, "What happened?" The injured guy said he went out, found tracks, followed tracks, and *bam!* got hit by a train.

STUFFED

Hunter Bob was visiting Hunter Sam and was given a tour of his trophy-filled home. In the den was a stuffed lion. Hunter Bob asked, "When did you bag him?"

His host, Hunter Sam, answered, "That was three years ago, when I went hunting with my wife."

"What's he stuffed with?" asked Hunter Bob.

"My wife!"

A HUNTER'S SCHEDULE

6:00 P.M.: Arrive at camp—see deer grazing.

6:01 P.M.: Load gun.

6:02 P.M.: Fire gun.

6:03 P.M.: One dead pickup.

6:05 P.M.: Hunting partners arrive in camp dragging deer.

6:06 P.M.: Repress desire to shoot hunting partners.

6:07 P.M.: Fall into fire.

6:10 P.M.: Change clothes, throw burned ones in fire.

6:15 P.M.: Take pickup, leave hunting partners and deer in camp.

6:25 P.M.: Pickup boils over due to holes shot in block.

6:26 P.M.: Start walking.

6:30 P.M.: Stumble and fall, drop gun in mud.

6:35 P.M.: Meet bear.

6:36 P.M.: Take aim.

6:37 P.M.: Fire gun, blow up barrel that's plugged with mud.

6:38 P.M.: Mess pants.

6:39 P.M.: Climb tree.

11:00 P.M.: Bear leaves. Wraps gun around tree.

12:00 A.M: Home at last. Fall on knees, thanking Maker.

WILD SHOTS

When he was fined for using last year's hunting license, Zeke claimed, "I was only shooting at the ones I missed last year."

He bought a hunting jacket with a Velcro closing. He accidentally rubbed up against a moose and got dragged through the woods for five miles.

"I'll never go moose hunting again. I didn't mind carrying the big gun, but the 200-pound decoy was a real drag."

One night a caveman comes running into his cave and says, "Whew! There was a tiger chasing me all the way home."

His wife asks why, and the caveman answers, "I didn't stop to ask!"

LICENSE OR NO LICENSE

A hunter just tagged his deer as the game warden walked up. "Where's your license?" asked the warden.

"Don't know," replied the hunter.

"Okay, you're under arrest for no license. Follow me to the road, and help me drag the deer," returned the warden.

"No way," answered the hunter. "You drag it."

Two hours later, after the warden had dragged the deer to the road, the hunter remembered which pocket held his license.

KIDS' HUNTING RIDDLES

Two fathers and two sons went duck hunting. Each shot a duck, but they shot only three ducks in all. How come?

The hunters were a man, his son, and his grandson.

What is the best way to hunt bear?

With your clothes off [bare].

MARTIAL ARTS

It's a known fact that one should be kind to those who practice martial arts. If they're happy, there's no kick coming. Milton Berle said that he practices an ancient martial art called Choo Dai Yuk. "When I'm attacked by an enemy, I scream. If that doesn't scare an attacker off, I go into my battle stance and kick, slash, and butt. If that doesn't take care of him, I go back to screaming."

BE A CHICKEN

So ya know, I've been taking these kung-fu classes lately. I must say, the teachers are great. They teach you how to be as power-ful as a tiger, as quick as a monkey, and as smart as a dragon. Why just the other day, these guys came up to me with a knife and demanded money. So, I turned chicken and ran!

KARATE KIDS

After four karate lessons, I can now break a two-inch board with my cast.

I have a black belt in karate. It's not that I'm good; it's just that I never wash it.

Karate makes sense. If you practice breaking boards in half, you'll be able to protect yourself the next time a board attacks you!

MILITARY ARTS

Did you hear about the idiotic karate champion who joined the army? The first time he saluted, he knocked himself out.

BLACK BELT MUSTS

Must be able to disable a man using only a Kleenex tissue as a weapon.

Must be able to catch a fly with chopsticks.

Must be able to change into a judogi in a phone booth at any given moment.

Must be able to sing Karaoke.

Must be able to fight blindfolded and win (against blind competitors, of course).

Must be able to choreograph street fights for Jackie Chan movies.

Must be able to keep all bleeding internal.

Must be able to trim an entire forest into a bonsai garden in twenty-five minutes or less.

MURPHY'S LAWS OF MARTIAL ARTS

Eight scientific principles that apply to the study of all martial arts.

1. The wimp who made it through the eliminations on luck alone will suddenly turn into Bruce Lee when you're up against him.

2. The referee will always be looking the other way when you score.

3. The day you leave work/school early to make it to class on time, the sensei will be sick.

4. The sensei will only use you during demonstrations for joint locking techniques.

5. If you have to use your training in self-defense, your attacker's father will be a lawyer.

6. After a flawless demonstration, you will trip on your way back to your seat.

7. After years of training without a single injury, you will pull a groin muscle the night before your black belt exam.

8. No matter how many times you take care of it before your promotion exam, you will invariably have to go to the bathroom when it's your turn.

TAKES THE CAKE

Then there's the poor karate black belt who broke his hand trying to cut a Christmas fruitcake in half.

KIDS' KARATE RIDDLES

What do you get if your sheep studies karate?

A lamb chop.

What would you get if you crossed a karate instructor with a wheelbarrow?

A chopping cart.

RACING

The popularity of this sport can hardly be overstated. Did you know that the word *race car* spelled backwards is "race car"? How many other sports can say that? And you didn't think NASCAR was educational. . . .

NORMAL VERSUS F1 CAR

Everyone knows that a regular car is better than a racing car for the following reasons:

- No door: For Pete's sake, any- one can climb in and steal it.
- No roof: Can't always have an umbrella at hand.
- No radio or CD player: How boring to drive close to two hours with nothing to listen to.
- No heating: Driver's toes must become very cold.
- No coffee cup holder: Those guys can spill hot stuff all over themselves, what with steering with one hand and trying to drink with the other.
- No windshield wipers: And they expect them to drive in the rain?

- No windshields: Guess this and the one above go hand in hand.
- No headlights: No wonder they only drive in the daytime.
- No turn signal: How can they indicate they intend to pass?
- Only one seat: How can a guy take his girlfriend for a date at the local drive-in?
- No anchor for a baby seat: And they try to make us believe that safety comes first?

KNOCK, KNOCK

Who's there?
  Cargo.
Cargo who?
  Cargo beep, beep.

FOR PARKING LOT JOCKEYS

Sometimes in the mall parking lot you think that NASCAR is in control. Here are a few tongue-in-cheek suggestions to make shopping center parking more competitive:

- When waiting for a parking spot, stop in the middle of the lane, don't signal, and maneuver your car into a diagonal position to prevent others from passing.
- Always park on the lines, taking up as many spots as possible. Diagonal parking is preferred.
- In a crowded parking lot, if you find a spot and have the opportunity to pull through to the adjacent one, drive up halfway and take up two spots by stopping between them both.
- If you have a handicapped license or tag, use up a regular parking spot.
- When a vehicle from the opposite direction is signaling and waiting for a parking space, position your car so that you are in his way and let the car behind you take it.
- Always leave your shopping cart behind or tightly parked between parked vehicles.

- When holiday shopping at the mall, which requires you to load your bags into the car and go back in to do more shopping, do *not* tell the driver who is sitting patiently, watching you load your car, and signaling for your spot.
- Park your humongous eight-cylinder gas-guzzler in a one and one-half spot labeled "Subcompact Cars Only."
- When loading your car in a parking lot, leave all the doors wide open and take your time when you see a car waiting to pull in an adjacent spot.
- If you don't see a speed limit sign in the shopping center lot, there isn't any limit!
- Finally, read the small print in your automobile insurance policy for verification that you are covered, "irregardless"!

Follow these suggestions to make your parking lot feel like a battlefield for a demolition derby.

MISQUOTE

Al Kulwicki, stock car racer, on racing Saturday nights as opposed to Sunday afternoons: "It's basically the same, just darker."

KNOCK, KNOCK

Who's there?
Carl.
Carl who?
Carl get you there faster than a bike.

YOU ARE PROBABLY A NASCAR FAN IF. . .

You spell NASCAR in Christmas lights on your roof in April.

You are sure that the last four words of the National Anthem are "Gentlemen, start your engines!"

You are able to recall every NASCAR driver and his car number, but you can't recall how old your kids are.

In the same light, you can remember the entire NASCAR schedule, but you have forgotten family birthdays, anniversaries, and the date you and your wife had your first date—at a NASCAR race.

Your wife's nickname is "Lugnut."

You change a tire faster than your baby's diaper.

OLD MAN ON A MOPED

A hip young man who is taken up by auto racing goes out and buys the best street car he can find that makes him feel like a NAS-CAR jockey. He finds the best and most expensive car in the world, a five hundred thousand dollar Cosmo Quad Turbo RX-7.

Driving it home, he stops for a red light, where an old man on a moped pulls up beside him. "What kinda car ya' got there, sonny?"

The young man tells him and adds, "It cost five hundred thousand dollars."

"Wow, that's a whole lot of money. Why does it cost so much?"

"Because the car can do up to two hundred miles an hour."

The moped driver asks, "Can I take a look inside?" The moped driver pokes his head in the window and looks around. Leaning back, he exclaims, "That's a pretty nice car, all right!"

Just then, the light changes, so the guy decides to show the old man how much speed the car has in it. He floors it, and within thirty seconds the speedometer reads 200 miles per hour. "This should show the old guy," the young man mumbles.

Suddenly, he notices a dot in his rear-view mirror. It seems to get closer, then *whooosh!* It whips past him going more than two hundred miles an hour. "What on earth can be going faster than me?" Then, ahead, he sees a dot coming toward him. *Whoooosh!* It goes by the opposite direction! It almost looks like the old man on his moped. "How could a moped out-run an RX-7?"

There it is, coming back toward him at full speed. "Oh no!" It plows into the new RX-7, demolishing the rear end. The young man jumps out and, to his absolute surprise, sees the old man on the moped, his head bleeding. "You're hurt bad," he says. "Is there anything I can do for you?"

The old man groans and replies, "Yes. Unhook my suspenders from your side window!"

NOT EXACTLY RACING

Sitting on the side of the highway waiting to catch drivers who use that stretch as a speedway, a state patrolman sees a small car putting along at twenty-two miles per hour. *This is dangerously slow to drive,* he thinks, turning on his lights and pulling the car over.

Approaching the auto, he sees that there are five wild-eyed old ladies as pale as ghosts. "Ma'am," he says to the driver, "how fast were you driving?"

"I was doing exactly the speed limit," the driver reported. "What seems to be the problem?"

"Ma'am, you weren't speeding, but you should know that driving slower than the speed limit can also be a danger to other drivers."

"Slower than the speed limit? No, Officer, I was doing the exact speed limit!"

The officer explains to her that twenty-two is the route number, not the speed limit. A bit embarrassed, the woman grins and thanks the officer for pointing out the error.

"Before I let you go, ma'am, I have to ask—is everyone in this car okay? These women seem awfully shaken."

"Oh, they'll be all right in a minute. We just got off Route 119."

PIT TALK

Q: Why did the bewildered racing car driver make ten pit stops during the Grand Prix?
A: He was asking for directions.

SPEED DEMON

A police officer pulls a guy over for speeding and has the following exchange:
Officer: May I see your driver's license, please?

Driver: I don't have one. I had it suspended
   when I got my fifth DUI.

Officer: May I see the owner's registration
   for this vehicle?

Driver: It's not my car. I stole it.

Officer: The car is stolen?

Driver: That's right. But come to think of
   it, I think I saw the owner's registration
   in the glove box when I was puttin' my
   gun in there.

Officer: There's a gun in the glove box?

Driver: Yes, sir.

   Hearing this, the officer immediately
calls his captain. The car is quickly sur-
rounded by police, and the captain approaches the driver to handle the tense
situation.

Captain: Sir, may I see your license?

Driver: Sure. Here it is. It's valid.

Captain: Whose car is this?

Driver: It's mine, Officer. Here's the
   registration.

Captain: Would you slowly open your
   glove box, please, so I can see if there is
   a gun in it?

Driver: Yes, sir, but there's no gun in it. See?

Captain: I don't understand it. The officer

who stopped you said you told him you
didn't have a license, stole the car, and
had a gun in the glove box.

Driver: Really? Ain't that somethin'? And
I'll bet the lyin' guy told you I was
speedin', too.

FREEWAY RACER

Ole got a new cell phone, and on his way
home on the freeway, he called his wife,
Lena.

"Hello, Lena. I'm calling you from the
freeway on my new cell phone."

Lena says, "Be careful, Ole. The radio
says that some nut is driving the wrong
way on the freeway."

Ole says, "One nut, my eye. There are
hundreds of them!"

BAD DRIVING

Three indications that your driving is not
up to snuff:

- You have a reserved parking space
  with your name on it at traffic
  court.

- Your family already has a road-side cross ready to mark the inevitable spot.
- Every time your cell phone rings while you're putting on your makeup, you spill your iced tea, drop your Game Boy, and rear-end the car in front of you on the freeway.

NASCAR EVALUATION

NASCAR would be more of a sport if half the cars were driving in the other direction.

KIDS' AUTO RIDDLES

What ten-letter word starts with g-a-s?
Automobile

Why is a violin like an auto?
It is best when tuned-up.

Why is an old car like a baby playing?
Because it goes with a rattle.

What did the jack say to the car?
"Can I give you a lift?"

Why did the farmer plant old car parts in his garden?

He wanted to raise a bumper crop.

RUGBY

You Americans have no idea how to play real football. In your Yankee way, you toss what you call a football around and attempt to keep away from as much bodily contact as possible. When a match is over, many of your players' uniforms are still clean and bloodless. Your footballers in their padding look like they were packed by Christie's, along with some Austrian crystal. And for that your boys earn tens of millions of dollars. So much for the Boston Tea Party!

BRIT HUMOR

Rugby Player: Doctor, doctor, every morning when I get up and look into the mirror. I feel like throwing up. What's wrong with me?

Doctor: I don't know, but your eyesight is perfect.

Q & A

Q: Why don't rugby players have midlife crises?

A: They stay stuck in adolescence.

Q: Why do rugby players like smart women?

A: Opposites attract.

PRONOUNCE THIS

Two rugby fans are arguing about how to pronounce the team name, Wigan.

Fan 1: I say it's Vigan.

Fan 2: No it's not, it's Wigan. I bet you five pounds I'm right.

Fan 1: Okay, you're on. I'll ask that man walking toward us. Excuse me, sir, my friend and I are having an argument. Do you say Wigan or Vigan?

Man: It's Vigan.

Fan 1: Ta, mate.

Man (walking up the street): You're velcome.

MOUTHY

It's been said that a certain Welch rugby player is so stubborn, he approaches every subject with an open mouth.

A CONTACT SPORT

A rugby player was badly hurt in a match. Both of his ears were ripped off. Between his club and his insurance company, the earless player received a huge money settlement, which he invested in a sportswear company.

The next day he set up three manager interviews. The first guy was great. At the end of the interview, the rugby player asked, "Do you see anything different about me?"

The interviewee responded, "Why yes, I can see you have no ears." This so infuriated the boss that he threw the man out.

The same thing happened at the second interview.

The third and last interview went wonderfully. Before offering the interviewee the job, the rugby player asked, "Did you notice anything different about me?"

To his surprise the man answered, "Yes, you wear contact lenses," causing the ex-rugby player to say, "What an incredibly observant young man you are. How did you know that?"

The young man started laughing and finally responded, "Well, it's pretty hard to wear glasses with no ears."

RUGBY SCRUBS

Why did the rugby player go to see the vet?
His calves were hurting.

Why didn't the bicycle play rugby?
It was too tyred.

Rugby player in a Chinese restaurant:
   Waiter, these noodles are a bit crunchy.
Waiter: That's because they're chopsticks, sir.

A man in pain went to the doctor.
Man: I've just been playing rugby, and
   when I got back, I found that when I
   touched my arm, my leg or my tummy,
   and everywhere else, it really hurt.
Doctor: Hmmm. I'd say you've broken
   your finger.

KIDS' RUGBY RIDDLES

If a rugby player gets athlete's foot, what does an astronaut get?

Missile toe.

What's a hardwood floor's favorite sport?

Rug-by.

SKATING

Funny the way most Americans (and others, for that matter) have become armchair figure skating judges. The average lady on the street is certainly able to tell an acceptable double axel from a not-so-hot lutz or salchow. And she's on a first-name basis with the Nancys, Brians, and Elvises of the sport. What she can't tell you is why her husband more often than not gets really angry when figure skating competition preempts the curling finals between Canada and some Balkan country.

THE CUTTING EDGE

Q: How is music like ice skating?
A: If you don't "C sharp," you'll "B flat."

While ice skating, my friend had a nasty fall, sliding downward twenty feet across the ice. The rink doctor rushed out and examined him and decided there was nothing he could do for the large bruise on his forehead. His solution: "Would you like some ice?"

LANGUAGE

Little Angie wanted to be as graceful and lovely as her beautiful figure skating idol Nancy Kwan. Her grandmother tried to convince her that the language she used was important to ladylikeness.

"My dear," she said, "there are several words in your vocabulary that are not ladylike. One is 'super' and the other is 'lousy.'"

"Oh," Angie replied, "tell me what they are. I won't use them anymore."

CLAWS

While examining a pair of new figure skates, neophyte skater Doug asked: "Hey, hold on. What do I do with these, uh, claws on the front of my skates?"

Walter replied, "Those are toe picks."

"Toe picks," Doug mused. "Let me guess, it has something to do with personal hygiene."

MOTHER CHAT

There is an Olympic champion skater whose mother is so proud of him. He goes to a psychiatrist every day and spends the whole hour just talking about her.

BUMPER STICKERS

Hockey Player in Trunk
Have Spins, Will Travel.
Hey Cutie, Your Rink or Mine?

SIGNS YOU'RE NOT A PERFECT 6.0

Judges can't tell the difference between you and the Zamboni.

Your coach is yelling, "Let go of the railing!"

You lutz yourself over the boards and into a hot dog vendor.

During a spin, your skate flies off and embeds itself in the judge's head.

Your costume looks an awful lot like your Denny's uniform.

You perform your long program to the theme from *The Dukes of Hazzard.*

You cut your program short because you have to return your rental skates.

You put the "cow" in salchow.

DUCK, GUYS

Ernie and Bernie put on their ice skates and ventured out onto the frozen lake. After skating in circles for a while, Ernie stopped and asked Bernie, "Do you think there are any ducks around here?"

"Of course not," answered Bernie. "They all flew south for the winter."

"Well, in that case," replied Ernie in a panicking voice, "I think the ice is quacking!"

THROUGH THE ICE

Even though it was winter, the ice on the surface of the pond wasn't yet strong enough to support skaters. Nevertheless, one young skater decided to try it. It wasn't long before there were cries for help from the direction of the pond. The farmer from the farm adjacent to the pond heard the young skater's cries and rushed to the pond.

The young skater, his teeth chattering, was shoulder-deep in the water. Putting a board across the ice, the farmer ventured out as far as possible and extended his arm, saying, "Work over to me and grab hold. I'll pull you out."

The young man pled, "I can't swim. Just throw me a rope."

"I don't have a rope. Look, you better come toward me. It don't matter if you can't swim. See, the water only comes to your shoulders."

The young man explained, "Look, it's ten feet deep. I'm standing on a fat guy who broke the ice!"

JUDGE NOT!

It was the Olympic men's figure skating competition. The first competitor on the ice was from Russia. His classical music accompaniment was beautifully interpreted, and he was well rehearsed, but there was no great artistic feeling in his moves. The judges presented their scores: Britain—5.8; Russia—5.9; United States—5.5; Ireland—6.0.

Next on the ice was the American competitor, causing no end of excitement in his sparkling stars and stripes costume. Skating to some rock and roll music, he got the crowd clapping. He skated with excitement, but not without a bit of hesitancy in his jumps. He missed landing a triple salchow and lost his center in a spin. After his turn, the judges flashed their scores: Britain—5.8; Russia—5.5; United States—5.9; Ireland—6.0.

The skater from Ireland made his entrance in a shoddy, tattered costume, with skates tied on his shoes. Reaching the center of the ice arena, he fell flat on his face, giving him a gushing nose bleed. He stood and tried to skate, but fell again. There was blood on his face, costume, and on the ice. Finally, slipping and crawling, he got himself off the ice. For the third time the judges declared their decisions: Britain—0.0; Russia—0.0; United States—0.0; Ireland—6.0!

The other judges turned to the Irish

judge and asked, with strong emotion, "How could you give that mess of a performance 6.0? Why did you do it?"

With not a sign of regret, the judge from Ireland turned to his colleagues and announced, "You've gotta remember, it's pretty slippery out there."

ICE SKATER

The wife and I were watching a figure skating show on television on which Dorothy Hamill was introduced. I commented on how young she looked. The wife said, "And why not? She's been on ice all her life."

KIDS' SKATING RIDDLES

What is the hardest thing about learning to skate?

The ice.

What is the hardest thing about learning to roller skate?

The floor.

Why shouldn't you tell a joke while you are ice skating?

Because the ice might crack up.

SKIING/SNOWBOARDING

One of the most practical uses of skiing was recently announced by the emergency room at a Squaw Valley hospital: "As of late, we have prepared a pamphlet that we distribute with each ski purchase. The title is, 'How to Convert Your Skis Into Leg, Arm, or Back Splints.'" In this same brochure the doctor/author admits that skiing can be a time-consuming sport. For every day on the slopes, you can spend seven in the hospital.

ONE-LINERS

A guy learning to ski remarked, "By the time I learned to stand up, I couldn't sit down."

Skiing: A winter sport that people learn in several sittings.

Sign at the foot of a ski run: Laws of Gravity Strictly Enforced.

Old skiers never die. They just go over the hill.

TRAINING FOR NEXT SEASON

Visit your local butcher shop and sit in the walk-in freezer for half an hour.

Soak your gloves and store them in the freezer after every use.

Fasten a small rubber band around the top half of your head before going to bed at night.

If you wear glasses, begin wearing them with glue smeared on the lenses.

Throw away a hundred dollar bill—now!

Walk across the neighborhood ice rink twenty times dressed in your ski boots, carrying two pair of skis and an accessory bag (which you drop every three minutes). Pretend you are looking for your car.

Place a small but angular pebble in your shoe, which you've lined with crushed ice, then tighten a C-clamp around your toes.

Go to McDonald's and insist on paying ten bucks for a hamburger. Be sure you're in the longest line.

Buy a new pair of gloves and immediately throw one away.

Fill a blender with ice, leave the lid off, and hit the pulse button. Let the spray blast your face. Leave the ice on your face until it melts. Let it drip into your clothes.

Dress in as many clothes as you can and then proceed to take them off because you have to go to the bathroom.

Slam your thumb in a car door. Don't go see a doctor.

Repeat all of the above every Saturday and Sunday until it's time for the real thing.

A SNOWBOARDING LESSON

As a mature man, supposedly with all my marbles, I learned to snowboard by the two-step method: Step One—Watch my teacher do something. Step two—Try to do the same myself.

I was pretty good at Step One. The problem with Step Two was that I had to perform all the feats on a snowboard, which turned out to be a violation of at least five important laws of physics. I'd struggle to my feet and attempt to stand. That's when the Physics Police dropped a huge chunk of gravity on me, and I hit the concrete snow, causing a near avalanche of the white stuff. If I hadn't gotten out of there, I'd have been completely covered.

I now realize that the small hills you see on the slopes are formed around the bodies of forty-seven-year-olds who tried to learn snowboarding.

Aftermath

This is my current breakfast menu: Black coffee and two-hundred and fifty aspirin. This is because I went snowboarding, where I was used as a trampoline by the Clydesdale horses.

SKIING POSTURE

I look around and watch young people skiing via the downhill method. I ski via the breath-catching method, in which you stand sideways on the slope, looking as athletic as possible without moving a muscle (which could cause you to actually start sliding down the hill).

If anyone asks if you're okay, you say, "I'm catching my breath!" in a tone of voice that suggests that at any moment you're going to swoosh rapidly downhill, whereas in fact you're planning to stay right where you are, rigid as a statue, until the spring thaw.

EQUIPMENT

In skiing, you wear a total of two skis, or approximately one per foot. This enables you to sort of maintain your balance by moving your feet. Plus you have poles with which you can stab people if they get in your way or make fun of you at close range.

A Skier's Glossary

alp: One of a number of ski mountains in Europe. Also a yelled request for help on the continent.

avalanche: An actual peril skiers face, frightening the timid away from the sport. See also: Blizzard, Death on the Slopes, First Aid, Fracture, Frostbite, Hypothermia, Lift Collapse.

bindings: Automatic mechanisms that protect skiers from serious injuries during a fall by releasing skis from boots, sending the skis skittering across the slope where they can trip two other skiers.

bones: There are two-hundred and six bones in the body. No need for worry: the two bones in the middle ear have never been broken while skiing.

cross-country skiing: Traditional Scandinavian all-terrain technique. Good exercise, cheaper than buying lift tickets, no lines.

exercises: A few simple warm-ups to get prepared: (1) Tie a cement block to each foot and climb a flight of stairs. (2) Sit on the outside of a fourth-story window ledge with skis on and pole on lap for at least thirty minutes. (3) Bind your ankles together, lie flat on floor; then, holding a banana in each hand, get to your feet.

gravity: One of the fundamental forces of nature that affects skiers. The other three are the strong force that makes bindings jam; the weak force that makes ankles give way on turns; and electromagnetism, which produces dead batteries in expensive ski-resort parking lots.

inertia: Tendency of a skier's body to resist change of direction or speed due to Newton's First Law of Motion: two objects of different mass falling side by side will have the same rate of descent, but the lighter one will have a larger hospital and home care bill.

skier: One who pays an arm and a leg for the opportunity to break them.

traverse: To ski across a slope at an angle. One of two quick and simple methods of reducing speed.

tree: The other method.

SKIING DEEP THOUGHTS

Then there was the dumb skier who got a nasty frostbite on his legs because he couldn't figure out how to get his pants over his skis.

All things are possible, with the exception of skiing through a revolving door.

Did you hear about the businessman charged with operating a monopoly? He had three ski lodges and a hospital.

A SKIER'S ROMANCE

He was a knockout on the ski slopes. His photo and stats appeared in *Sports*

Illustrated. Those who knew him couldn't figure out why he was still single. He found it impossible to make a date. He'd start to talk to a girl on the slopes or in the lodge, and his tongue would twist up like a pretzel. His close friends tried to encourage him. "Read some self-help books," they urged.

So he went to a local bookstore and looked for a volume that might do the trick for him. On the nonfiction shelves, he spied a book titled *Ways to Women.* Paying for the book, he rushed home, only to discover that he'd bought volume ten of an encyclopedia.

KIDS' SNOW RIDDLES

What is plowed but never planted?
  Snow.

Where do snowflakes dance?
  At the snow ball.

SOCCER

Soccer moms are big news today. Politicians refer to them as regular middle-class voters who have nothing better to do than cart the kids off to the nearest park practice field. Dads don't seem to get that same kind of credit. One of the kids playing in such a league was asked by her dad how the game went. The little daughter answered, "It would have gone better if the other team would just learn how to share." See, there's Mom's influence again.

HEAD SHOTS

Millions of people play soccer because that way they don't have to watch it on television.

Soccer players do better academically than football players because soccer players use their heads.

Q & A

Q: Who are the most indispensable men in international soccer?
A: The riot police.

Q: What has twenty-two legs and says,
   "Crunch, crunch, crunch"?
A: A soccer team eating potato chips.

Q: What position did Dracula play on his
   soccer team?
A: Ghoulie.

Q: What were the soccer star's first words
   as a baby?
A: "Look, Ma, no hands."

Q: Why do soccer players have so much
   trouble eating popcorn?
A: They think they can't use their hands.

JUNGLE GAME

It was a boring afternoon in the jungle, so
the elephants decided to challenge the ants
to a game of soccer. The game was going
well, with the elephants beating the
mighty ants ten goals to zip, when the ants
gained possession.

The ants' star player was advancing the
ball toward the elephants' goal when the
elephants' left back came lumbering

toward him. The elephant trod on the little ant, killing him instantly.

The referee stopped the game. "What do you think you're doing? Do you call that sportsmanship, killing another player?"

The elephant sadly replied, "I didn't mean to kill him—I was just trying to trip him up."

REF WORK

Referees at British matches always have a particularly hard time. One poor unfortunate, officiating at his first tussle, was checking in with the team managers before the kickoff.

"Well, that seems to be about everything," said the boss. "Now if you'll just give us the names and addresses of your next of kin, we can start the match."

BRITISH FOOTBALL

Q: What part of a football [soccer] pitch smells nicest?
A: The scenter spot!

Q: Why aren't football stadiums built in outer space?

A: Because there is no atmosphere!

Q: What do a footballer and a magician have in common?

A: Both do hat tricks.

Q: Which goalkeeper can jump higher than a crossbar?

A: All of them. A crossbar can't jump!

Q: Why are football players never asked out to dinner?

A: Because they're always dribbling.

ANOTHER ONE

"Just a minute, ref," yelled the goalkeeper. "That wasn't a goal."

"Oh, wasn't it?" shouted the referee. "You just watch Sports Report on television tonight!"

LOCKER-ROOM SIGHTINGS

His body belongs to a religious group—the Hairy Krishnas.

He's so hairy his knees have bangs.

He was never worried about his baldness. He was born that way.

His hair is getting thinner—but who wants fat hair?

I've seen better bodies than his on used car lots.

He's so tall, six months a year he goes around with snow on his head.

His teeth protrude so. When he smiles, he combs his mustache.

OUCH!

In a far-off eastern country, the game of soccer was the most popular sport. Everybody played it, even the royal family. But one day, the king died, and a new king took his place. The new king hated soccer and outlawed it, so all the games had to be abandoned. *Reign* stopped play.

THE GIFT

The newlywed wife of a soccer player said to the clerk in the sports shop, "I'd like a hat trick, please."

"A hat trick?" he replied, mystified.

"It's for my husband's birthday," she answered. "It's something he's always wanted."

HECKLER

The crowd was mercilessly jeering and heckling the referee in a high-school match. Finally, the poor official walked over to the bleachers and sat down next to his loudest critic.

"What are you doing?" asked the spectator.

"Well," said the ref, "It seems you get the best view from here."

KIDS' SOCCER RIDDLE

What game do girls dislike?

Soccer [sock her].

SWIMMING

Competitive swimmers are a breed unto themselves, what with their flesh-colored nose clips, fetching caps, and matching Speedos. In the first place, who'd be caught dead in that skimpy outfit, which is reminiscent of an old knock, knock:

KNOCK, KNOCK

Who's there?
Panther.
Panther who?
Panther no panth, I'm going swimming!

Knock, knock
Who's there?
Dwayne.
Dwayne who?
Dwayne de pool, I'm dwowning!

Knock, knock
Who's there?
Thatcher.
Thatcher idea of a dive?

THAT'S NOT FUNNY

Boy: Mom, why can't I swim in Loch
    Ness?
Mother: Because there are monsters in it.
Boy: But Daddy's swimming in it.
Mother: That's different. He's insured.

AH, INSPIRATION

Two frogs fell into a deep cream bowl.
    One was an optimistic soul.
But the other took the gloomy view.
    "We'll drown," he lamented with
    much ado, and with a last despairing
    cry, he flung open his eyes and said,
    "Good-bye."
Quoth the other frog with a steadfast grin,
    "I can't get out, but I won't give in,
I'll just swim around till my strength is
    spent,
    then I'll die the more content."
Bravely he swam to work his scheme,
    and his struggles began to churn the
    cream.
The more he swam, his legs aflutter,
    the more the cream turned into butter.
On top of the butter at last he stopped,
    and out of the bowl he gaily hopped.

What is the moral?
*It's easily found—if you can't hop out,
keep swimming around!*

Q & A

Q: Why do you keep doing the back-
   stroke?
A: I've just had lunch, and I don't want to
   swim on a full stomach.

Q: Did you hear about the slow swimmer?
A: He could only do the crawl.

Q: Dad, there's a man at the door collect-
   ing for a swimming pool. What should
   I give him?
A: Give him a bucket of water.

Fun for a Swimming Pool

Stand on top of the high board and say
you won't come down until your demands
are met.

Ask people if they've seen your pet shark.

Ask an attractive lifeguard to practice CPR on you.

Sit at the top of the water slide and don't move.

Insist that you saw a monster at the bottom of the pool.

Sing and dance on top of the diving board, then do a belly flop as your grand finale.

Play Marco Polo by yourself.

QUESTION

If one synchronized swimmer drowns, do the rest have to drown, too?

NONSWIMMER

Elmer: Waiter, waiter! There's a dead fly swimming in my soup.
Waiter: Nonsense, sir. Dead flies can't swim.

A man in a swimming pool was on the very top diving board. He poised, lifted his arms, and was about to dive when the attendant came running up, shouting, "Don't dive! There's no water in that pool."

"That's all right," said the man. "I can't swim."

KEEP AN EYE

"I thought I told you to keep an eye on your cousin," the mother impatiently barked. "Where is he?"

Well," her son replied thoughtfully, "if he knows as much about canoeing as he thinks he does, he's out canoeing. If he knows as little as I think he does, he's out swimming."

KIDS' SWIMMING RIDDLES

If you were swimming in the ocean and a big alligator attacked you, what should you do?

Nothing. There are no alligators in the ocean.

Is it dangerous to swim on a full stomach?
Yes. It is better to swim in water.

Why did they throw the elephants out of the swimming pool?
Because they couldn't hold their trunks up.

Why shouldn't you listen to people who have just come out of the swimming pool?
Because they are all wet.

What would you get if you crossed a movie house and a swimming pool?
A dive-in theater.

TENNIS

A popular nonathletic humorist is credited with comparing tennis with bowling. He claims to have lots of fun bowling because you can enjoy yourself even if you stink. Not so tennis. He claims that every decade or so he attempts to play a match. That match generally consists of thirty-seven seconds of actually hitting the ball and two hours of yelling, "Where did the ball go?" "Last time I saw it, it was sailing over that condominium," and so forth. With bowling, once you let go of the ball, it's no longer your legal responsibility. They also have these wonderful machines that find your ball for you and send it right back.

DISTAFF TENNIS

My wife always hits the ball into the net on her first serve. She doesn't want to get cheated out of a second shot.

Ella: I just adore tennis. I could play like this forever.
Fella: You will, if you don't take lessons.

FACTS

There are supposed to be three million tennis players in the United States.

Actually, there are nine players. The rest are waiting for a court.

Tennis champs are getting so young they give autographs in crayon.

The Russians took up tennis about twenty years ago. They already play a good game at the *nyet*.

SHORTS

Anyone who can leap a three-foot net after a match should take up track and field.

Today's tennis pros are so young they give autographs on an Etch-a-Sketch.

Age has no bearing whatsoever on your tennis game. It just keeps you from winning.

TENNIS Q & A

Q: What did one tennis ball say to the other tennis ball?
A: See you 'round.

Q: What's a horse's favorite sport?
A: Stable tennis.

Q: Why did the elephant float down the river on his back?
A: So he wouldn't get his tennis shoes wet.

TENNIS ADVICE

To err is human. To put the blame on someone else is doubles.

Never marry a tennis player, because to him love means nothing.

KNOCK, KNOCK

Who's there?
Tennis!
Tennis who?
Tennis five plus five.

A CONTACT SPORT?

Two men were warming up to play tennis when one man noticed that the other had bruised shins. "Those look like they're in pretty bad shape. You play hockey, too?"

"No," replied the other man, "bridge. I just trumped my wife's ace."

KIDS' TENNIS RIDDLES

What is the loudest sport?
Tennis, because everyone raises a racquet [racket].

What can you serve but never eat?
A tennis ball.

At what sport do waiters really excel?
Tennis. They really know how to serve.

Why were the tennis players arrested?

Because they were involved with racquets [rackets].

TRACK/FIELD/OLYMPICS

It isn't a coincidence that the thinly clad runners and nimble field event practitioners have become the symbols of the modern Olympic movement. It has to be a throwback to those glorious days when Greeks from Athens to Zakynthos ran and tossed and jumped for the love of sport and for the glory of a laurel leaf garland. How appropriate that today's Olympic hero runs and tosses and jumps for the love of endorsements.

OLYMPICS

Three non-Olympians are trying to sneak into the Olympic Village to scoop souvenirs and autographs.

The first says, "Let's watch the registration table to see if there's a crack in the security system that we can use to scam our way in."

Immediately, a burly athlete walks up to the registration table and announces, "I'm Angus MacPherson, Scotland. Shot put." He opens his gym bag to display a shot to the registration attendant.

The attendant says, "Very good, Mr. MacPherson. Here is your packet of registration materials, complete with hotel keys, and other info."

Hot dog! The first guy grabs a small tree sapling, strips off the branches and roots, walks up to the registration table, and says, "Chuck Wagon, Canada, Javelin."

The attendant says, "Very good Mr. Wagon. Here is your packet of registration materials, hotel keys, passes, meal tickets, and so forth. Good luck!"

The second guy grabs a street utility manhole cover, walks up to the registration table, and introduces himself, "Dusty Rhodes, Australia. Discus."

The attendant says, "Terrific, Mr. Rhodes. Here is your packet of registration materials, hotel keys, a full set of passes, and meal tickets. Enjoy yourself."

The two guys scamper into the village but suddenly realize the third guy is missing. They groan, "Oh no!" Guy three was the kind of a guy who could get himself in trouble out of pure ignorance. He could blow their cover.

At last they spot him walking with a roll of barbed wire under his arm. He walks up to the registration table and states, "Foster Bean. Blue Eye, Missouri. Fencing."

RUNNING RIDDLES FOR ADULTS

How do you start a firefly race?
   Ready, set, glow!

Why did the English bald man take up running?
   To get some fresh 'air.

Why do elephants wear running shoes?
   For running, of course.

BOSTON MARATHON

Did you hear about the two fat men who ran in the Boston Marathon? One man ran in short bursts, and the other in burst shorts.

CROSS COUNTRY

You might be a cross country runner if. . .

- Your toenails are black.
- Your shoes have more miles on them than your car does.

- You need a magnifying glass to see your name in the paper.
- You have chafing in strange places.
- People say, "You run three miles—all at one time?"
- You run farther in a week than your bus travels for meets.
- The most enjoyable time you've had all month is a day off from practice.
- You can spit and run at the same time.
- You can eat your weight in spaghetti.
- You eat spaghetti three times a day.
- You debate the advantages of antiperspirant versus deodorant.
- You schedule dates around meets.
- You wake up every morning in pain.
- Gatorade is your drug of choice.
- Your Saturdays for the next four years are ruined.
- You can see your ribs through your shirt.
- You have to run around in the shower to get wet.
- You call bus seat seventeen your second home.
- Your dessert is brussels sprouts.

100-METER

Two girl sprinters are training for the 100-meter race. One says to the other, "You won't believe this, but I've just run 100 meters in ten seconds."

The other says, "But that's impossible; that's the world record."

"Nah," the other answers, "I took a shortcut."

BELIEVE IT OR NOT

Did you hear about the hopeless athlete? He ran a bath and came in second.

LADIES AND GENTLEMEN

The prime minister of a well-recognized country is opening the Olympic Games and has to read a speech.

"Oh," he says. "Oh, oh, oh."

An aide nudges him. "Mr. Prime Minister, stop," he says. "You're reading the Olympic symbol."

A LIMERICK

A javelin thrower called Vicky,
Found the grip of her javelin sticky.
When it came to the throw;
She couldn't let go;
Making judging the distance quite
tricky.

POLE VAULTER

At the recent Olympics, a man was walking through the Olympic Village carrying a long pole. A reporter came up to him and asked, "Are you a pole vaulter?"

The surprised man answered, "No, I'm a German. But how did you know my name is Walter?"

OLYMPIC VIEWS

Did you hear the one about the guy who won a gold medal in putting the shot at the Olympics? He had it bronzed.

Len: What would you get if you crossed a computer, a slob, and an Olympic athlete?
Ben: A sloppy [floppy] discus thrower.

Did you hear about the music lover who tried out for the Olympics? He's a compact disc thrower.

Biff: Coach, where am I on the Olympic tug-of-war team?
Coach: You're the third jerk from the left.

OLYMPIC TORCH PROBLEMS EN ROUTE

Budget cuts cause torch to be replaced by less-than-dependable Bic lighter.

Difficulty getting melted marshmallows off torch after s'mores party.

Running seven miles before realizing the torch is still in the 7-11 restroom.

One really disgusted Smokey the Bear.

First-degree burns to runners unfamiliar with how to "receive the baton."

Torchbearers driven insane by repeated playings of the "Chariots of Fire" theme.

Torch-jackings in urban areas.

Male runners repeatedly get lost and refuse to stop for directions.

KIDS' RUNNING RIDDLES

What is the difference between a racer and a locomotive engineer?

One is trained to run, the other runs a train.

How do chickens start a race?

From scratch.

OTHER STUFF

This is the catch-all, what-did-we-miss-in-the-earlier part of this collection.

Here's a cute one: A pastor skips service one Sunday to go bear hunting in the mountains. As he turns a corner along the path, he and a bear collide. The pastor stumbles backwards, slips off the trail, and begins tumbling down the mountain with the bear in hot pursuit. Finally, the pastor crashes into a boulder, sending his rifle flying in one direction and breaking both of his legs. The pastor is lying there; he's lost his gun, and the bear is coming closer, so the pastor cries out in desperation, "Lord, I repent for all I've done. Forgive me for not being in church. Please make this bear a Christian." The bear skids to a halt at the pastor's feet, falls to his knees, clasps his paws together, and says, "Lord, I do thank you for the food I am about to receive."

CHESS PLAYERS

A group of chess enthusiasts checked into a hotel and were standing in the lobby discussing their recent tournament victories. After an hour, the manager came out of the office and asked them to disperse.

"But why?" they asked as they moved off.

"Because," the manager explained, "I can't stand chess nuts boastin' in an open foyer."

CHESS Q & A

Q: What's the difference between a chess player and a man who is broke?

A: One watches his pawns; the other pawns his watch.

SKYDIVING

If at first you don't succeed, skydiving is definitely not for you.

SEASONS

Teacher: Name the four seasons.

Jock: Baseball, basketball, football, and hockey.

SWING ON THIS

Chuck: Did you hear about the trapeze
performer who fell to the ground?
Buck: Did he hit a net first?
Chuck: Yes, and Annette wasn't too happy
about it.

TIME ON YOUR HANDS

"I bet I can run faster than you can,"
bragged Hank to Frank.

"I bet you can't," replied Frank.

To prove his point, Hank took Frank
to the roof of a thirty-story building. Hank
removed his watch and dropped it over the
edge of the building. Quickly, in a whirl of
dust, Hank dashed down the stairs. Reaching the ground floor, he reached out his
hand and caught the watch.

Signaling it was his turn, Frank
removed his watch and let it fall. Taking
his time, he strolled to the elevator and
pushed the button. A few minutes later,
the elevator appeared and Frank stepped
in. After stopping at several floors, he
arrived at the lobby, stepped out, and
calmly walked outdoors just in time to put

out a hand and catch his watch.

"Hey, that was amazing!" remarked Hank. "How did you do it?"

"Simple," said Frank. "My watch is five minutes slow."

ATHLETIC $-$-$

I know a Texas athlete who has bookcases just for his bankbooks.

A certain pro ballplayer is so rich that his bills are big enough that we don't have presidents for them.

MORE $-$-$

One of those fat-cat wealthy athletes took his wife to dinner at the fanciest restaurant in Paris. As two headwaiters hovered over them, Mrs. Rich Athlete said, "Honey, order the most expensive thing you can think of, and order it in a loud voice so everyone will know just how rich we are."

Mr. Rich Athlete took a sip of water and yelled to the head waiter, "BRING ME THREE HUNDRED DOLLARS WORTH OF FRENCH TOAST AND FRIES!"

POOR GRANDPA

Cindy: I can't believe you took your blind grandfather skydiving.

Mindy: He really enjoyed it.

Cindy: Do you plan to do it again?

Mindy: No way.

Cindy: But he liked it. Why not?

Mindy: Well, he enjoyed it, but his guide dog wasn't too crazy about it.

VARSITY IQ

Did you hear about the athlete who was so dumb that when he earned his varsity letter, someone had to read it to him?

AN OBSERVATION

A small girl watching a water-skier said to her father, "That man is so silly. He'll never catch that boat."

TRUE COMMENTATORS' MESS UPS

Identities are eliminated to protect the not-too-innocent:

- It's a great advantage to be able to hurdle with both legs.

- We now have exactly the same situation we had at the start of the race, only reversed.

- I was in a no-win situation, so I'm glad that I won rather than lost.

- There's going to be a real ding-dong when the bell goes.

- There is Brendan Foster, by himself, with twenty thousand people.

- The lead car is absolutely unique, except for the one behind it, which is identical.

- And with an alphabetical irony, Nigeria follows New Zealand.

- Just under ten seconds for Nigel Mansel. Call it 9.5 in round numbers.

- And here's Moses Kiptani—the nineteen-year-old Kenyan who turned twenty a few weeks ago.

- The French are not normally a Nordic skiing nation.

- That's inches away from being millimeter perfect.

- Bobby Gould thinks I'm trying to stab him in the back. In fact, I'm right behind him.

- I'll fight Lloyd Honeyghan for nothing if the price is right.

- If history repeats itself, I should think we can expect the same thing again.

- The Queen's Part Oval, exactly as its name suggests, is absolutely round.

OTHER SPORTS RIDDLES

What is in your arm and in the sea?
A muscle [mussel].

What does an umpire do before he eats?
He brushes off his plate.

Where is the headquarters for the Umpire's Association?
The Umpire [Empire] State Building.

What season is it when you are on a trampoline?
Springtime.

Why did the tightrope walker always carry his bankbook?
In order to check his balance.

What game do you play in water?
Swimming pool.

What kind of car drives over water?
Any kind of car, if it goes over a bridge.

SIGNS OF THESE TIMES

Only in sports-crazy America. . .

- Can a half-time pizza get to your house faster than an ambulance.
- Are there handicapped parking places in front of a skating rink.
- Do fans order double cheeseburgers, large fries, and a diet Coke at the concession stand.
- Do we leave cars worth thousands of dollars in the driveway and put our useless junk in the garage.
- Do we buy hot dogs in packages of ten and buns in packages of eight.
- Do we have drive-up ATM machines with Braille lettering.

Free Raft

Seems that a few years ago, some unnamed Boeing employees decided to "borrow" a life raft from one of the 747s. They were successful in getting it out of the plant and home.

When the guys took it for a float trip of the Stilliguamish River, they were quite surprised by a coast guard helicopter that was homing in on the emergency locator that is automatically activated when the raft is inflated.

The "borrowers" are no longer employed at Boeing.

Bad Sky Diving

Alfred is a daredevil, so he decides to go skydiving for the very first time. After listening to the instructor for what seems like days, he is ready to go.

Excited, he jumps out of the airplane. About five seconds later, he pulls the ripcord. Nothing happens. He tries again. Still nothing. Alfred starts to panic, but remembers his backup chute. He pulls that cord. Nothing happens. He frantically begins pulling both cords, but to no avail.

Suddenly, he looks down, and he can't believe his eyes. Another man is in the air with him, but this guy is going up! Just as the other guy passes by, the totally scared skydiving Alfred yells, "Hey, do you know anything about skydiving?"

The other man yells back, "Are you kidding? Do you know anything about lighting gas stoves?"

SKYDIVER VERSUS GOLFER

What is the difference between a bad golfer and a bad skydiver?

A bad golfer goes, Whack! *"Doggone it!" A bad skydiver goes, "Doggone it!"* Whack!

HER PLACE

On her way back from the concession stand, Julie asked a man at the end of the row, "Pardon me, but did I step on your foot a few minutes ago?"

Expecting an apology, the man said, "Indeed you did."

Julie nodded and noted, "Oh, good. Then this is my row."

HALFTIME ENTERTAINMENT

The band had just finished its under-rehearsed selection and received a big ovation from the stands. A woman in the front row stood up and shouted, "Play it again! Play it again!" The band director and drum majors all bowed directly to the woman. Then she yelled, "Play it again until you get it right!"

Q: How do you make a bandstand?
A: Take away their chairs.

Did you ever see some of those marching bands? The way they play, it's a good thing they keep marching.

MIAMI TEAM MEMBERS

Where else but in Miami can you see a football team dreaming of a tan Christmas?

The quarterback checked into a Miami hotel and said, "Please wake me at seven." The clerk replied, "The receptionist doesn't get in until eight. Maybe you could wake her."

EXERCISE QUICKIES

I don't believe in jogging. When I die, I want it to be from an illness.

I can do everything today that I could do when I was nineteen. Can you imagine what rotten shape I was in when I was nineteen?

I may not jog or play tennis, but I'm a very brisk eater.

SPORTS ERRATA

One Midwestern newspaper told about an athlete who "was at death's door until Dr. _____ pulled him through."

A tall, lanky basketball player screamed because an item indicated that he'd died. The athlete threatened to sue, but the editor promised to make up for the mistake. The next day the man's name was listed in the birth announcements.

A sports doctor was speaking to the team about anatomy. To help the men remember, he gave a fast quiz at the end of the session. One of the answers that came in was, "At the end of the stomach you have the bowels. There are five of them—*a, e, i, o, u*—and sometimes *y.*"

In the same exam (see above), this answer was written: "Gender tells you whether a man is masculine, feminine, or neuter."

Artificial perspiration is how you make a person live when he just died a minute ago.

FINANCES

Michael Jordan has no folding money. His wad is so big he can't bend it.

The teacher asked, "How many make a million?"

Little Pete answered, "Playing basketball or football?"

Money really isn't that important. Is a quarterback with fifty-million dollars happier than a pitcher with forty-million dollars?

ATHLETIC ROMANCE

A shot putter got beat up for kissing the bride after the ceremony. Of course, it was three years after the ceremony.

Rumor has it that a well-known coach is so in love with himself that every time he passes the mirror in his office, he asks, "Who is fairest of us all?"

TEAM ACCOMMODATIONS

Baseball roomies stand at the hotel registration desk. "Would you like a room with a tub or a shower?" they were asked.

"What's the difference?"

"Well, with a tub you sit down."

Shortstop Sid: These bellhops love to gather tips. I once ordered a deck of cards, and the bellman made fifty-two trips!

Halfback Hal: Service was the slowest in this hotel. If you ordered room service, you had to leave a forwarding address.

Forward Freddie: It really was a suspicious hotel. The Gideon Bible was on a chain.

Caddy Carl: My room wasn't bugged, but the bed was.

SPORTS MEDICINE

A burly professional wrestler was sitting in a doctor's office and kept mumbling, "I hope I'm sick, I hope I'm sick." Another waiting patient asked why he wanted to be sick. The wrestler replied, "I'd hate to be well and feel like this."

The college jock sat on his doctor's examination table explaining the pain in his arm. The doctor asked, "Did you ever have this before?" The young athlete admitted that he did, to which the doctor answered, "Well, you've got it again."

A doctor phoned a patient, "Your check came back." The patient said, "So did my tennis elbow."

Coach Chuck: My doctor wears a mask because of his fees.

The Sport of Marriage

A man and his wife were arguing over who should brew the coffee each morning.

The wife said, "You should do it because you get up first, and then we don't have to wait as long to get our coffee."

The husband said, "You are in charge of the cooking around here, so you should do it. It's your job, and I don't mind waiting for my coffee."

Wife replied, "No, you should do it, and besides, it's in the Bible that the man should do the coffee."

"I can't believe that," responded the husband. "Show me."

So she fetched the Bible, opened it to the New Testament, and showed him that at the top of several pages, it indeed says HEBREWS!

A Sport?

Did you hear about the sword swallower who swallowed an umbrella? He wanted to put something away for a rainy day.

PLAY TIME

Logan knocked on the front door of his friend Burt's house. When the mother of the boy answered the door, Logan asked, "Can Burt come out to play?"

"No," answered the mother, "it's too cold."

"Well then," said Logan, "can his ball glove come out to play?"

STADIUM PARKING

I remember the good old days when it cost more to run a car than to park it.

I just bought a raffle ticket. The second prize is a car. The first prize is a parking space.

I saw a ballpark parking lot the other day just filled with compacts. Of course, they weren't like that when they came in.

PARTNERS

The three partner/owners of a major league ball team were on their way to an out-of-town business meeting when one of the partners gulped and told the second partner, "I forgot to lock the safe."

The third partner said, "There's nothing to worry about. All three of us are here."

VIEW BLOCK

We took our seats in the stadium, sat back, and waited for the game to start. However, fate was against us. A couple sat down in the seats directly in front of us. Both were tall, but the man was immense. His shoulders blocked out my wife's whole view of the playing field. After straining to find a view to the left or the right, my wife tapped the lady in front and said, "Could you bend him in half?"

ICING RELATIVES

We have so many relatives dropping in on us, I had to hire a hockey goalie to guard the icebox.

RITZY SPORT

There's a certain overpaid athlete who has been living so high on the hog that he won't eat ladyfingers unless they're manicured.

The same guy's so ritzy the bags under his eyes are Gucci and he's developed Perrier on the knee.

FAME

At lunch, several on-the-rise professional athletes began to discuss what fame is. One thought that athletes like them were the most famous people in the country. The second agreed, but added that it was television coverage that made them famous. The third, a basketball player named Miller, said, "I'll tell you exactly what fame is. Let's say I were to go to Rome at Easter. Pulling strings, I would get into the Vatican. A million people are gathered in St. Peter's Square. Then there's a roar, and the massed crowd looks up at a balcony, from which hangs a great banner. Several men appear, among them me. I'm standing right next to the Pope. Now, if somebody points and asks the person next to him, " 'Who is that man next to Miller?', that's fame!"

KIDS' OTHER RIDDLES

What is a mosquito's favorite sport?
Skindiving.

How many people can you fit into an empty sports stadium?
One. After that it's not empty.

Do Eskimos go on safaris?
Not safaris I know.

If you enjoyed

THE GOOD SPORTS JOKE BOOK,

look for these other hilarious titles from
Barbour Publishing!